LOST IN LOGISTICS

A step-by-step guide to transform your board and get your ministry moving

By Bob Moss

Warner Press Inc.
Warner Press and "Warner Press" logo are trademarks of Warner Press, Inc.

Lost in Logistics
A step-by-step guide to transform your board and get your ministry moving

Scripture quotations used in this book were taken from the following:

Requests for information should be sent to:

Warner Press Inc
2902 Enterprise Dr
P.O. Box 2499
Anderson, IN 46013
www.warnerpress.org

Editors: Karen Rhodes, Tammy Tilley
Designers: Curtis Corzine & Katie Miller

ISBN: 978-1-68434-085-9

Printed in USA

warner press®

MADE IN THE USA

With candor and leadership savvy, Bob Moss provides a most helpful narrative within the wider context of congregational decision-making structures. His experienced-based applications are testimonials to the organizational clarity and effectiveness that are possible for pastors, boards, and congregants. Read, apply, and streamline your congregational energies to engage more fully in the church's mission.

—Joseph Cookston, Ph.D.
Former Executive Pastor, Salem Church of God, Clayton, Ohio

As chair of our local church board, I had the opportunity to participate in the implementation of a governance board under the leadership of Pastor Bob Moss. The result of this decision and process has been transformative. Effective governance is at the very root of a healthy church. We continue to reap tremendous benefit years later. Many thanks to Bob Moss for creating this resource for the local church.

—Dr. David E. Cox
Board Chair, Salem Church of God, Clayton, Ohio

Bob Moss has written a book that is a must-read for pastors looking to implement a healthy, growth producing structure in the local church. Bob was the Lead Pastor of the church I currently serve and I'm living with the leadership structure that he created. This is not just a book of difficult to implement ideas. I can tell you from personal experience what you will find in this book absolutely works!

—David Colp
Lead Pastor, First Church, St. Joseph, Michigan

It is easy to draw a yawn when you breathe the words "structure" or "organization" into a crowd. But, when reviewing history—especially New Testament history—it is clear that structure and organization are front and center in getting good things done. From the feeding of the five thousand, to the calling of the Twelve, to the sending of the Seventy, Jesus was an organizational genius. From the Jerusalem Council to the deacons appointed to manage material relief in the early church, the Holy Spirit paid close attention to the church's structure. In this book, Bob Moss pours his heart into helping us understand the link between ministry and organizing principle. Never imagine that how things are set up is incidental to what gets done. The Spirit moves across these pages even as He moves across churches who are organized for miracles. Which brings us back to the feeding of the five thousand; and, to this must-read for every church leader. Pick it up. Read it. Put it into Practice. Watch God work.

—Jim Lyon
General Director, Church of God Ministries, Anderson, IN

For two amazing congregations and their dedicated leaders who have journeyed with me in the quest of a better way to fulfill the ministry of Jesus. I am forever grateful to the people of First Church of God, St. Joseph, Michigan and Salem Church of God, Clayton, Ohio for trusting me to be their pastor and for giving me freedom to lead.

CONTENTS

INTRODUCTION

For more than a decade, I have been asked to consult with congregations about their bylaws and decision-making structure, and I've been asked by pastors and church leaders to put my thoughts about church governance into writing.

The model of church governance described in this book has become widely accepted among congregations, and many books describe the theory of governance. Several of these books, formal training in governance, and personal experience have contributed greatly to *Lost in Logistics*. While not attempting to create another textbook on the subject, I am hoping to offer this book as a practical implementation manual for pastors and church leaders.

The principles shared in these pages have been growing in my life and ministry over time. My friend Rod Stafford first introduced me to a new way of thinking about church bylaws and structure in the late 90s. We've walked this journey together. At his invitation, I became one of the first nonresident board members to sit with his leaders, and to be given full voting privilege as a member of the Advisory Council of Fairfax Community Church in Fairfax, VA. It was an amazing privilege to be a part of the leadership group for nearly twenty years as the congregation grew from three hundred to over twenty-three hundred in weekend worship services.

These principles have been employed in two congregations I've served as senior pastor. Both the First Church of God in Saint Joseph, Michigan, and the Salem Church of God in Clayton, Ohio, have greatly benefited from the structural changes described in this book. The standards described will work in any size congregation.

As a reader you should know that I am writing as a brother in Christ, one who has spent a life in pastoral ministry. The principles of leadership I'm sharing are time-tested and have produced extraordinary results for many congregations. I feel compelled to share these thoughts in order to set your church free from being lost in a maze of logistical decisions.

The church has unwittingly paralyzed itself by accepting unnecessary limitations. People have become weary with endless meetings and complex decision-making processes. Many younger leaders turn their backs in disinterest to the endless cycles of committees and meetings that have defined church life for generations. There is a better way!

I discovered that I first had to train myself in matters of church governance, and then begin to train the leaders in the church. The simple fact is, we've stumbled along for far too long without a thorough understanding of effective church board training and leadership principles. I want to help.

I've been around church boards all my life, directly and indirectly. My grandfather was my childhood pastor, and my father was a member of the board of trustees in that small church. When I was eleven, we moved to another community and began attending the largest church in the small town of Newton Falls, Ohio. Through the years, my father was often the chairman of the church board and also served as chairman of the building committee when a major new building addition was added to the facility. My mother served as chairperson of the Christian education committee in that church. Consequently, I saw my parents spending many evenings after work in meetings at the church.

Our family was at the church on Sunday mornings for worship, Sunday night for evening services, Wednesday night Bible study, and Thursday night choir practice. Committee meetings were interspersed in between the regular church gatherings. The church was central in our family's priorities, but at times I remember my parents' weariness too.

By the time I was in high school, I began to listen more attentively to my dad's description of things discussed in the meeting of the board of trustees. I remember how, even then, I was sometimes puzzled by what day-to-day management issues the board considered. Much time seemed to be lost in unnecessary conversation over trivial matters. From what I heard, the church was trying to manage day-to-day operations from the board level rather than allowing the staff to do its work.

My own foray into church governance proved no better. In my mid-twenties I had accepted the role of solo pastor in a small congregation in Washington state. Board meetings were long, boring, and exasperating. The treasurer actually brought the stack of bills to the board meeting where a separate motion was made for each individual invoice to be paid! Every insignificant matter concerning the facility, the church program, and the schedule was discussed and voted upon. Purchases larger than $500 required a vote of approval from the entire church.

Like many pastors, I was resigned to the routine of regular and ineffective board and committee meetings. I was frustrated, but so were the lay leaders of the church. The introduction of a healthier and more appropriate way of making decisions and guiding the ministry was like a drink of cool water to a thirsty wayfarer in a desert of dysfunction.

When I proposed new methods of church governance to First Church in St. Joseph, Michigan, and the Salem Church in Clayton, Ohio, I was elated by their affirming response. We made changes slowly, methodically going through the process. We scheduled multiple question and answer sessions and patiently answered concerns. As a result, the new bylaws and new system received a strong endorsement vote (in the high ninetieth percentile) in each congregation. This is even more notable when considering that each congregation had deep historic roots. One was founded in 1895 and the other in 1909. Rather than being resistant to these changes, they accepted them enthusiastically. Each congregation has thrived and grown in response.

The chapters of this book will be testimonial, experiential, and aimed at helping others apply this system to their congregations. The Church of God, of which I'm a part, needs a new standard for healthy congregational structure, and I'm indebted to Warner Press for their enthusiastic encouragement of this project.

This clear governance system will work in small churches as well as large. It's a principle-based system that makes clear who is responsible for specific decisions in the church. Some decisions are made by the entire congregation—those are important—and six of them are listed. Some decisions are made by the governing board, while still others are made by the staff. When clarity exists about who makes various decisions, life is really good. Conflict lessens and collaboration increases.

Many years ago, prior to the bylaws change in our Michigan congregation, I met a leader leaving the church building as I was entering. I could tell the young woman was a bit upset so I asked, "Is everything okay?"

She bristled somewhat and said, "There is so much red tape in this church that before any decision can be made, it has to pass through three or four levels of committee bureaucracy for approval, and I'm just frustrated!"

This woman and her husband worked for a ministry called Young Life. That ministry did not operate with layers of committees and bureaucracy. She was really frustrated because she desired to see some forward progress in certain ministries in the church, but she realized decisions were majorly bogged down in the approval process.

For leaders like her, and for every pastor who desires to lead an effective, energized board, I say, "There is a better way!"

Bob Moss
2018

CHAPTER 1

Exploring Reasons Why Church Leaders Are Frustrated

It's no secret that church leaders are frustrated with how decisions are made in the church. Each month, dedicated men and women spend countless hours away from their homes and their families seated at a meeting table somewhere in the church. Sadly, they often return home fatigued, uninspired, and wondering why their effort seemed so pointless.

When I was a pastor, it dawned on me that I lacked training in effective board leadership, and when I realized that most individuals who sit on church boards have not received training either, I decided I needed to look for a solution. This book is meant to share insights I have gained in my personal journey. I want to help train pastors to train their church leaders in effective church governance and move from a sense of futility and frustration to purposeful leadership. Through the years I've noticed how dedicated church leaders will persevere in the midst of meeting weariness because they love the church, are loyal to the pastor, and most of all feel impelled by their love for Christ to serve. I'm convinced by my experience that I can help you make the transition from being weary and unfulfilled in meetings, to feeling joyful and energized by effective, visionary meetings.

Insight is gained by taking a look at the agenda of the average church board or committee meeting. Are you convinced the discussions and the decisions being made have any lasting impact? Often, the items on the agenda are not the appropriate subjects for the board or committee to address. We're missing the target. We're aiming too low. We're not talking about the needs we should be meeting in the community. Instead, we discuss administrative and management matters like carpet replacement or restroom remodeling. It all feels rather pointless. There must be a better way.

Is it possible for the ministry of the church to be outwardly focused? Do our leaders discuss what's happening in the community that cries out for the hands of Jesus to help? What about the opioid crisis, for instance? Are we doing anything about that? Is there a crisis in foster care for children as a byproduct of the drug crisis? Have we opened the doors and invited our neighbors in for a community forum in which people can talk about the needs they are seeing in the neighborhood? Do we believe that every time we demonstrate the love of Jesus to others in the community we are literally pushing back the darkness with the light of God's love?

When the board meeting agenda calls us to focus only on church administrative business, we are aiming too low. Church business has its place and is important. But most important is the gospel that calls us to focus on the needs within our community and to prayerfully strategize to meet those needs.

In the following pages we will explore the reasons why church leaders are so frustrated and lost in the logistics of church life. It's only as we understand the frustration that we are able to make a better plan as we go forward.

Frustration Number One:
Too many meetings

Having too many meetings is the first among all the reasons that church leaders become frustrated with church life. I'm fairly certain that most people do not drive home from work saying, "Oh boy! I get to go to a committee meeting at the church tonight!"

It's easy to recognize people's weariness of too many meetings by their body language. They show up for a committee meeting, and you know they would rather be somewhere else. Anywhere else. Committees meet because the bylaws prescribe a monthly meeting. Yet, often the committee assembles, and the chairperson says, "I didn't print an agenda, because there is really nothing to discuss tonight." Even still, the meeting drags on for sixty to ninety minutes while the group discusses the "nothing" that isn't printed on an agenda.

Later in these pages, I will suggest a better way for ministry groups to meet. I propose that many committees be reconstituted as ministry teams, that the presence of these teams be deleted from the bylaws, and that the gates of membership on teams be opened to allow people to serve according to their calling. When ministry teams meet on an "as needed" basis rather than the once-a-month time prescribed by bylaws, it dramatically changes the chemistry and effectiveness of the group. Released from required minutes, reporting, and voting, the group can begin to function as a true ministry team. When people get to use their gifts in ministry, it all starts to become fun and fulfilling once again.

Even the governing board of the church will benefit from a reduced meeting schedule. When the business of the church is reviewed on a quarterly basis rather than a monthly basis, a bigger perspective is achieved and the tendency of the board to speak into day-to-day operational affairs is minimized.

Frustration Number Two:
Lack of clarity about who is empowered to make certain decisions

Frustration mounts when church committees burn precious hours talking but without a clear agenda or purpose. Then, when the need for a decision is finally presented, the committee will defer the decision to yet another board or committee because it is unclear who is empowered to make a final decision. It's like a game of badminton when the subject is batted around relentlessly. This is a big deal. Church life suffers because capable leaders are no longer willing to be a part of a dysfunctional system.

Consider the frustration of youth group volunteer leaders in the following scenario: Justin (not his real name) approaches the chairman of the board of trustees asking for some additional funds to pay for the rental of the winter youth retreat site. When the budget was originally passed, the youth leaders were unaware the camp had increased the rental rate. The trustee chair advises Justin that he needs to be sure the youth event is approved by the church council. The trustee chair is aware that the date for the proposed youth group retreat conflicts with a big all-church anniversary celebration. Justin immediately contacts the chair of the church council to inquire about whether or not to change the retreat but is told that he needs to set up a meeting with the pastor to receive approval for the youth group and the adult leaders to be absent from the anniversary celebration. Justin is obviously frustrated as his request is being passed from one decision maker to another. Similar scenarios are repeated throughout the year as volunteer leaders attempt to navigate the maze of voices involved in decision making. Add to this the delays caused by the monthly schedule of board and committee meetings and one can imagine the arduously slow process in achieving a decision. For this and other reasons, many volunteers are opting out of church leadership when there is such lack of clarity and empowerment in decision making.

Frustration Number Three:
Difficulty filling all the committee slots required by bylaws

I've consulted with churches whose bylaws require so many positions to be filled that some adult leaders are committed to serving on multiple boards or committees. One congregation had a Sunday morning worship average of 140 (including adults and children) and the bylaws required 67 positions to be filled. Obviously, there were not 67 capable and qualified adults available to serve in these positions. As a result, the most capable leaders were involved in multiple boards and committees in the church. Meeting fatigue was negatively affecting their joy in serving.

When I was called to serve a Michigan church, I discovered the requirement of many boards and committees listed in their bylaws. There was a church council comprised of representative members of various ministries and other boards, a board of trustees which managed the property and the finances, a board of Christian education overseeing the choices of curriculum and the recruitment of teachers, a music and worship board that worked on the music schedule and the environment of the sanctuary, the board of outreach and missions concerned with outreach locally and the support of missionaries abroad, a youth ministry board planning the activities and schedule of a burgeoning youth group, a pastor-church relations board dealing with personnel issues, job descriptions and evaluations, and a nursery center board, overseeing the daily preschool ministry consisting of over 150 preschoolers in the program. In addition, there were several standing committees. There was an audio-visual aids committee, a faith promise committee, and a Christian action committee overseeing benevolence. There was also an active Women of the Church of God group. Each of these groups required elected officers and some level of input and guidance from the senior pastor. This organizational system required a large number of individuals to be placed on the annual ballot. Since meetings for each of the groups were scheduled on a monthly basis, it required many evenings spent at a church classroom table each week.

In those days, there was a large bulletin board near the fellowship hall where the minutes of each of the boards and committees were posted each month. Over time, in the midst of meeting fatigue, I began to wonder if we had become lost in logistics. It seemed the church had begun functioning like a legislative body with various boards making decisions, sometimes in unintended conflict with decisions of other boards, and often resulting in stalled momentum and gridlock. I began to ask myself, "Are we here to do ministry or make minutes?" Other times I asked, "Are we all about making disciples or making decisions?" The result was fatigue in keeping all the ministry slots filled, and it was draining the energy of the church. People were losing interest in participating in a system filled with an endless cycle of monthly meetings, but little forward progress. We urgently needed to discover a better way.

Frustration Number Four:
A tug-of-war between two boards

There was once a commonly held belief in church culture that if new believers or people new to the congregation were to become fully involved in the life of the body, they needed to become a part of a board or a committee in the church. The thinking seemed to be that by serving in the decision-making life of the church, a sense of belonging was nurtured. This value system provided a suitable environment for the proliferation of boards and committees to accomplish the ministry of the church. After all, the committee system provided an onramp for more and more people to become involved. Unfortunately, the tension and church politics surrounding much of a board or committee's work becomes discouraging rather than edifying to the new individual added into the mix. Too often we've seen people back away from the church after being exposed to well-intentioned people getting involved in meaningless discord. In my view, one disillusioned new believer is one too many.

One of the major by-products of this system is the creation of an environment in which two boards or committees can easily get into a tug of war over the sharing of financial resources, volunteer personnel, or the events calendar. It is not hard to imagine the frustration that ensues when one ministry board envisions a new program or initiative requiring funding, and a finance group refuses to support it. Tension such as this offers ripe opportunity for conflict in the church.

Whenever two boards are speaking into a directional decision, it offers a perfect setup for a struggle. That's another reason why church leaders get frustrated.

Pastor Larry Osborne, senior pastor at North Coast Church in Vista, California, describes the problem this way:

> I once thought the problem was sin and pride. The way I saw it, church boards were notorious for fighting because so many board members were carnal. The solution was simple: Get people right with God, and conflict will cease.
>
> But I've come to realize that sin and pride aren't always the key players. In fact, some of the most significant causes of conflict are sociological, not spiritual. For the most part, our board members were good and godly folks who sincerely wanted to know and do

God's will. The problem was, we had unwittingly structured ourselves for confrontation and division. Our systems and traditions were sabotaging our unity.

Once I saw how these structural roadblocks were hindering our effectiveness and unity, I began to identify and remove as many of them as possible. The results were dramatic. Posturing and infighting began to be replaced by a spirit of teamwork and cooperation. And a board that was once unable to agreeably purchase tablecloths and tires learned to tackle successfully the truly significant issues of ministry.[1]

Frustration Number Five:

A representative council may not have the perspective necessary for weighty problems

In the two-board system consisting of a church council and a board of trustees, the council is typically made up of chairpersons of the various committees and ministries of the church—for instance, the chair of the Christian education committee, the missions committee, the youth ministry committee, and so on. While this arrangement provides for information-sharing and calendar coordination, it does not necessarily mean the church council members see themselves as the spiritual eldership of the church body.

Early in ministry I discovered that the members of the council felt incredibly uncomfortable with some of the weighty spiritual or moral issues with which we had to grapple from time to time. In one particular meeting we had to deal with something that was a heavy spiritual issue in the church. I literally noticed how people shifted in their chairs. Their body language seemed to communicate, "I'm not comfortable with this discussion. I didn't sign up for this!" The unfortunate result of the two-board system meant that the church was devoid of any official spiritual leadership to advise the lead pastor in the difficult issues. Congregations with this structure must consider whether or not they have identified and empowered the spiritual leadership of the church. A reporting session for the various ministries serving as the church council does not provide for a wise group of leaders to partner with the pastor in giving spiritual direction for the forward movement of the church.

1 Larry W. Osborne, *The Unity Factor: Getting Your Church Leaders Working Together,* vol. 20, The Leadership Library (Carol Stream, IL: Christianity Today, Inc., 1989), 24.

Larry Osborne notes:

> Many churches have opted for the representative model. It fits well with our American democratic principles, as well as one of our most cherished doctrines, the priesthood of believers. It insures that everyone has a chance to be heard, not just those who are powerful or well-connected. And it is one way to guarantee the board stays in touch with the needs of the congregation.
>
> But in a board of representatives, the emphasis on representing various interest groups makes it difficult to justify keeping anyone off the board. From a representative perspective, any church member, no matter how divisive, has a right to lead.
>
> It's also harder to come to a consensus when faced with controversial issues. By definition, a representative board seeks to protect minority opinions; this often results in a stalemate rather than a solution.
>
> Finally, members of a representative board can start to see themselves as lobbyists. Jack may become the champion of traditional worship, while John defends the youth. Meanwhile, Susan fights for the rights of the Sunday school. Forgotten in the fray can be the most important thing: finding and carrying out God's will.
>
> For these reasons, and others, I've become a strong advocate of a leadership-oriented board. Rather than figure out what everybody wants them to do, the members of a leadership board have only one focus: finding the best course of action and following it. When faced with a difficult decision, they ask first not "how will people react?" but "what does God want us to do?"[2]

2 Larry Osborne, "Stopping Conflict Before It Starts" in *Leading Your Church Through Conflict and Reconciliation: 30 Strategies to Transform Your Ministry*, ed. Marshall Shelley (Minneapolis, MN: Bethany House Publishers, 1997), 79-80.

Frustration Number Six:
Pastor seems like a lobbyist seeking permission rather than a leader

Many years ago, I attended a leadership seminar in which a very well-known presenter instructed pastors on the art of navigating through board decisions. He gave the illustration of the key influencer of the board. While not the official leader of the church, he's the one to whom all board members look. If an idea is presented and he's nodding in affirmation, all others will vote to approve. If, however, he expresses disapproval by word or in posture, the idea is certain to be defeated.

The presenter went on to instruct pastors on the art of gaining pre-approval of ideas before the meeting. He said, "Take the man to coffee. Pitch your proposal. Gain his support in advance so that you can have assurance of the board's compliance when the meeting is in session."

For many years I thought this was an excellent idea! But over time it began to dawn on me how dysfunctional that "system" really was. Ideas did not rise or fall upon their own merit, but according to my ability to "schmooze" with the opinion influencer. I further realized that this was a dysfunctional behavior and could easily lead to manipulative behavior. What truth underlies the need to "win approval" from those whose opinions are valued? It's the reality of the disempowered pastor. It is in this environment that the pastor tends to operate like a lobbyist, seeking permission and approval from those who can easily withhold it. It gives the leadership of the church not to the shepherd called by God, but to those who feel they must protect the congregation from pastoral leadership that may be ineffective. As we continue in the step-by-step explanation of how to create a healthy decision-making culture in the church, I will present the plan for pastoral effectiveness, informed by the insightful and collaborative work of spiritually mature and capable board members.

Frustration Number Seven:
Bylaws often don't reflect the most dynamic ministries

Another reason church leaders are frustrated is that the bylaws don't reflect the most dynamic ministries. Many believe the bylaws need to list every ministry of the church.

That would be a false belief in my view. Let's say that a new ministry is launched that's reaching out to the neighborhood, to the community, and it's really growing. In time, it becomes the most dynamic ministry of the church. Soon it becomes obvious that the leadership of the new effective ministry does not have a seat on the council. Why? Because it's not mentioned in the bylaws.

In my view, all of the ministries of the church don't need to be mentioned in the bylaws. The purpose of bylaws is to clarify how decisions are made and who leads the direction of the church.

Frustration Number Eight:

Board members lack training or understanding of their roles and responsibilities

There is no doubt that one of the most neglected areas of training in the Christian church is the training of persons to serve on the governing board of the congregation. Without this training and orientation, each member of the board brings to the group his or her own prejudice and experiences as a frame of reference. Undoubtedly this results in frustration for pastors and board members alike. In my pastoral experience I've listened to lots of commentary from board members who think our church board should function similarly to whatever group they've had experience with, be it a school board, a commercial business, a fortune 500 company, or a government office, just to name a few.

Looking back over my life experiences serving on boards of various kinds, I realize that only two of the boards I served went through orientation and training. One training event was given when I served on the board of trustees of a small Christian college. The second training event was provided for those of us who served on the Ministries Council of our national church General Assembly.

In the latter part of my pastoral ministry at the Salem Church of God, we added an orientation session to the meeting of the board of elders once each year. This provided vital training to incoming elders as well as a refreshing of operating principles and values to ongoing members. In our journey from understanding the frustration of leaders to the implementation of a healthier decision-making structure, I will present a description of what a board is as well as what a board is not. We will consider what a board must decide as well as what a board must not decide. Training and orientation that bring clarity to these elements of decision making are key towards the achievement of health in the entire congregational system.

Author Charles Olsen describes the fallout of untrained boards:

> Have you ever thought about what happens to former church officers? After hearing lay leaders say about their term, "I'm glad it's almost over" or "Whew, I made it" or "Never again," I began asking why. I also noticed that a significant number of former church officers became inactive or dropped out of the church.
>
> - Recently, *Set Apart Lay Leaders*, a project aimed at revitalizing church boards, polled more than 600 board members. Nearly a third—29 percent—indicated they left "tired, weary, and burned out." They had come asking for bread and were given a stone.
> - One board member said, "The last three presidents of the church board in our church have dropped out of activity in the church within six months of their term."
> - Another said, "We were looking for three new council members and went through sixty-three names before we heard our third yes."
>
> What frustrated them about serving on the church board? Here are some comments that reveal deep frustration.
>
> - "How burned out I feel. My last year was my most unproductive one."
> - "How secular it is. We spend more time discussing leaky toilets than why our church is slowly dying due to no growth or vision."
> - "The lack of interest in pursuing God together. Prayer is a formality, not a way to seek his purpose and plan."
> - "The lack of concern for seeking Christ's guidance versus following our own personal agendas."
> - Can serving on a church board truly be life-giving instead of life-draining? Can board meetings actually become "worshipful work"? [3]

Having come to some level of understanding about why church board and committee leaders are weary and frustrated, let's move toward step two and the realization that there is a better way!

3 Charles M. Olsen, "A Kinder, Gentler Board Meeting," in *Growing Your Church through Training and Motivation: 30 Strategies to Transform Your Ministry*, ed. Marshall Shelley, vol. 4, Library of Leadership Development (Minneapolis, MN: Bethany House, 1997), 167–168.

CHAPTER TWO

Understanding the Hallmarks of Healthy Decision Making

Understanding is the second step towards creating a better decision-making culture. There are a number of resources that have greatly expanded my own understanding. I highly recommend the book *Free to Lead*, by Pastor Rod Stafford from Fairfax Community Church in Fairfax, Virginia. He's led his congregation through a significant transition in how the governing board functions. In fact, it was serving on the advisory council with Rod that first began to really sensitize me to the need for a better way in my own pastoral ministry.

When the Fairfax Community Church was running about 300 in attendance, the governance changed to the system I'm describing for you. Much growth in the congregation can be attributed to streamlined lines of authority in leadership and clarity in staff roles and responsibilities. Rod has coined the term "collaborative hierarchy." In this process we know who has the ultimate responsibility for decisions, yet many people collaborate to share their perspectives so the best decisions are made. Does that make sense to you?

I've also been influenced by a book called *Winning on Purpose, How to Organize Congregations to Succeed in Their Mission* by John Edmond Kaiser. It's an excellent book, and I've shared this with some of the lay leaders in my pastoral ministry. Kaiser's analogy of a sports team presents a good way to understand governance.

Perhaps the most central text on policy governance is written by John Carver, *Boards that Make a Difference—A New Design for Leadership in Nonprofit and Public Organizations.*

I had the opportunity to go through governance training in Atlanta, Georgia through the Carver Governance System. John and Miriam Carver have spent much of their lives training people and nonprofits how to lead with a governance model rather than a management model of decision making.

Another helpful resource is a book entitled *Governance As Leadership—Reframing the Work of Nonprofit Boards*. There's a wide field of study that can be utilized to acquaint yourself with a new way of thinking about governance. What I'm trying to do is to give you a testimonial and helpful perspective that has lots of handles for your use in implementing a healthy structure.

The authors describe an important shift in how the culture expects an effective leader to perform. "Constituents expect nonprofit CEOs to articulate clearly and persuasively the organization's mission, beliefs, values, and culture. Both the process and the substance should galvanize widespread commitment toward these ends. With input from stakeholders inside and outside the organization, leaders are expected to shape agendas, not impose priorities; to allocate attention, not dictate results; and to define problems, not mandate solutions. These expectations we now have for leaders closely resemble conventional notions of governing."[4]

While the church differs in many ways from other nonprofit organizations, the clearly changing trend of the past generation is that the senior pastor must be able to function very similarly to the CEO of other nonprofit organizations.

All of the training received, books read, resources reviewed, and personal experiences have helped me understand the common principle of decision making embraced in every instance. It is best described in these eight simple words:

Pastor—Leads

Staff—Manages

Board—Governs

People—Minister

In many churches, however, the roles and responsibilities are confused. Many times it appears that the pastor and staff minister, the congregation governs, and the board leads and manages. This flawed approach is in direct contradiction with the teaching of Scripture. The Apostle Paul's letter to the church at Ephesus reminds the church that the pastors are to equip God's people for ministry: *So Christ himself gave the apostles, the prophets, the evangelists, the pastors and teachers, to equip his people for works of service, so that the body of Christ may be built up* (Ephesians 4:11-12, NIV).

In the early days of church history, clarification was needed regarding who was to accomplish the ministry of the Word of God and who was to manage the daily details. It is described in Acts chapter 6:

4 Richard Chait, William Ryan, Barbara Taylor, *Governance as Leadership, Reframing the Work of Nonprofit Boards, BoardSource,* John Wiley & Sons, Inc., 2005, 3.

So the Twelve gathered all the disciples together and said, "It would not be right for us to neglect the ministry of the word of God in order to wait on tables. Brothers and sisters, choose seven men from among you who are known to be full of the Spirit and wisdom. We will turn this responsibility over to them and will give our attention to prayer and the ministry of the word (Acts 6:2-4, NIV).

Some may argue that the decision-making system I am describing gives all the power to the pastor. To the contrary, the pastor is given both responsibility and authority, is free to exercise leadership, but is also accountable to the governing board, which in turn, is accountable to the congregation.

The following organizational chart clearly communicates the concept.

Overview of the Governance / Accountability System

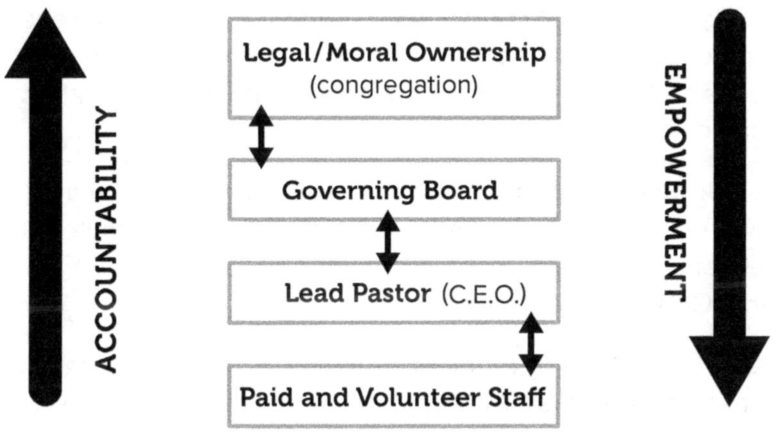

In this illustration, lines of accountability flow upward while lines of empowerment flow downward. This creates health through both accountability and empowerment. Everyone needs to be accountable to someone. Leadership without accountability eventually creates anarchy and chaos. This is why it is so important for the board and pastor to work together to gain a common understanding of mission. The overarching mission of the church was given to us by Jesus in Matthew 28:19: *Therefore go and make disciples of all nations, baptizing them in the name of the Father and of the Son and of the Holy Spirit, and teaching them to obey everything I have commanded you. And surely I am with you always, to the very end of the age.* While the central mission of the church is to bring the gospel to others everywhere and to teach them to obey Christ's commands, there are specific gifts and abilities imparted in the midst of congregations that will influence and shape each body's ministry in the world.

The governance model of decision making brings powerful help for staying on course. Once the board embraces the centrality of the great commission, coupled with the congregation's resolve to use its giftedness in reaching specific needs in the community, the church's ministry can begin gaining new ground in effectiveness. For instance, one congregation views its mission as ensuring the good news of God's grace is presented to every child and parent in our county.

The existence of many competing demands and expectations underscores the necessity of a clearly defined sense of purpose that can be clearly articulated by the lead pastor. It cannot be emphasized too strongly that the leadership of a local church must be clear about the purpose and God's specific calling for the local church. One of the things that I believe stalls us out as churches is that we don't spend time asking the question, "What is it that God is calling us to do at this time, in this community, with our particular resources?"

If we don't ask that question, then we're really aiming at nothing. A few years ago when I was pastoring at the Salem church near Dayton, Ohio, I spent a weekend with the board and we were focusing on that question. What is it that God's calling us to do?

I won't give you a moment by moment overview of the whole weekend, but I want you to know that the awareness came upon us that there were no congregations in proximity to us that had a dynamic ministry to children, or that were really leading children to Christ effectively.

We admitted that our own ministry was not very effective, and our ministry to children and their families was faltering. This admission changed our focus as a church. It changed how we staffed the ministry, too. In gathering facts, I had a conversation with the director of the local YMCA, a Christian man, active in the community. I asked him if he knew of any churches in our community that were extremely effective in reaching children and their families. He shook his head and said, "Sadly, no." This was just one more confirmation that we were hearing God calling our congregation to reach children in our community.

It cannot be emphasized too strongly how powerful it is that we become clear about what God is calling our church to do.

I was given the assignment to diligently work on finding the right kind of pastor to develop a vibrant children's ministry. I am happy to tell you that the Salem Church went from 35 kids in the church to well over 200 children in the church today. I recently visited this former pastorate and was told that every Sunday they're checking in new families who are bringing their children to church for the first time.

Again, this is what can happen when a pastor and board ask, "What is the main thing that God's calling us to do in our ministry?"

One biographer gave an example about the power of clearly defined purpose. He said Ronald Reagan was a president who had two objectives so clearly defined they could be written on the back of a business card: Defeat communism and lower taxes. Two phrases are still remembered as being emblematic of those two objectives. The first is from a speech at the Berlin Wall. "Mr. Gorbachev, tear down this wall!" The second is a term that became widely used, "Reaganomics." Both of these were clear echoes of a clearly defined purpose. This illustration is meant to underscore the fact that Ronald Reagan knew what he was about, and those were the two things that he wanted to accomplish.

In church life, the existence of many competing demands and expectations underscores the necessity of a clearly defined sense of purpose in the heart of pastors and leaders.

This is where the leadership board needs to work most closely with the lead pastor of the church in defining what is it that God's calling the church to accomplish.

We must be clear in understanding what competing demands and expectations are. Consider a university president. It's a very hard job with many constituencies grappling for their piece of the action. Take for instance, the sports program. Recruitment dollars, sports facilities, and equipment are hugely expensive. Then there are the demands and expectations of the university board. There are different demands and the expectations of the donor base, and still different demands and the expectations of the students. Let's not forget the demands and expectations of the parents of the students as well as the demands and expectations of the alumni. I can go on to list faculty, campus staff, government regulations, and financial institutions. Each of these bring expectations to bear upon the university president.

Another leader who faces similar competing demands and expectations is the president of a hospital. We can list patients, doctors, nursing staff, corporate donors, government regulators, insurance regulators, hospital visitors, security personnel and many others, all with competing demands and expectations.

The pastor of a congregation faces similar pressures due to competing demands and expectations borne of generational differences, musical preferences, staffing concerns, financial standards, community expectations, and so much more.

This reminds us of why we must be clear about who we are and what we are called to do because we are not going to be able to meet all of the demands and expectations. Trying to do so will only water down or dissipate a leader's effectiveness. It's the difference between looking through a rifle scope or looking through a kaleidoscope. One brings things into sharp focus. The other gives you a multifaceted colorful experience but there's no focus.

As a wise board and pastoral team regularly revisit and clarify the sense of purpose for the congregation, the question is asked, "What is God calling us to accomplish in this community to serve as Jesus would?" These statements are called ends.

In policy governance training, understanding the end result is paramount. They ask questions like: What benefit, for whom, at what cost? That's how you define what an end is. What benefit, for whom, at what cost? The lead pastor of a church should seek the input of the board in identifying the next critical success factors or imperatives that the ministry must address. Seeking to identify the ends to be accomplished causes you to identify any obstacle or problem that can obstruct the progress of the ministry. When I went to be the pastor at the Salem Church, I hired a coach to help me, because the coach asked me insightful questions. We had a meeting every week for an hour on the telephone.

My coach asked me this question: "What is your critical success factor?" I told him I wouldn't even know one if it grew in my front yard. He said, "Well, let me define what it is." He continued, "There is something or maybe it's a series of somethings that's holding you back as a church. And until you address it you'll always be held back. So, what is it?" This meant that I had to spend a lot of time in prayer. And a lot of time in meditation asking the question, "What's holding us back, Lord?" And you won't believe this, but it was a very abstract thing that the Lord helped me to identify.

It's easier if it's a very concrete idea like building a bigger sanctuary. That's a very concrete idea. But this was a very abstract idea. Over time I came to realize that the church was paralyzed by a scarcity mentality. And if you understood the history of that particular congregation, you would know that they had to navigate some pretty precarious financial challenges over the years.

When they moved out to the 65-acre parcel where they are now located, they had built a huge auditorium seating close to 2,000 people. Through some unfortunate circumstances and tough economic times, they came within a hair's breadth of losing the entire campus. A number of people in the church went out and remortgaged their houses and brought the money into the treasury of the church. They literally resolved the church's financial crisis by taking on another 20-year mortgage personally. That's what they did. That's pretty committed, to have your home paid off and to go remortgage it and give the money to the church. This was how committed some people were. But the unintended consequence was that some in the church began to see themselves as the providers, instead of God.

At that time funds were very, very limited. I felt that my spiritual role was to lead them into a provision mentality. I'm not using the word abundance, I'm using the word provision. So, we began some experiences in being focused on God's provision. Every week, we got the report on what the weekend offering was.

I would lead the staff in a prayer. "Thank you, God, our provider." And in every way, we began to acknowledge that God was a provider for the church. Today the church is fully funding their budget and is keeping ample funds in reserve to help them navigate the ups and downs of seasonal income.

It's really a miracle how it all happened. I could go on and write more of the story, but I'm trying to illustrate what happens when you get focused on recognizing the critical success factor that's holding the ministry back. You could also call it an imperative that's holding your ministry back. An imperative simply must be addressed in order for the ministry to move forward.

Without a healthy structure by which a pastor and board can focus on these things, you'll always be spinning your wheels in committee process. I'm hoping to build your understanding that a visionary board will make all the difference coming alongside pastoral staff to win the community for Christ.

Sadly, in the Church of God and in other church groups there are few examples of this kind of leadership being taught. Little by little, we're gaining some ground. In the past few years many of our churches are adopting the system of church governance and accountability. A short history lesson describing how so many congregations became entrenched in one way of thinking may be helpful.

Look at the Historical Perspective

In 1927, the Gospel Trumpet Company produced a book by Russell Byrum called *Problems of the Local Church*. His book was an attempt to address a prevailing difficulty in the Church of God movement, which had arisen with a strong anti-organization bias. The movement in its first forty years was very free-wheeling. Most congregations associated with the movement lacked structure. To answer the need, the book addressed all sorts of organizational and structural challenges facing the congregations across the movement. For several generations his book was viewed as the standard for church governance. In the preface he states:

> Since human church organization began to be repudiated a generation ago, local congregations of the Church of God have rapidly multiplied throughout the world. These have been confronted with many problems in the course of their development both as to their ecclesiastical and business affairs. In attempts to meet these problems young and inexperienced persons have too often introduced practices which were in conflict with sound doctrine. The need of a book dealing with the principles and practices of the local church in the light of the New Testament has long been felt. This work is an attempt to supply that need.[5]

In my own wide-spread journeying across the church, including the churches that I've led, I've discovered that this model from 1927 has been the prevailing model. Much has changed in our culture in a century. For instance, when that book was published, not everybody had a car in which to come to church.

But if they did have transportation, they might have had a Model-T Ford. There was no such thing as online meeting. There were no telephones, or fax machines, or internet. The world has completely changed, and the ways we're able to function in leadership positions are very, very different.

5 Byrum, Russell R., *Problems of the Local Church: A Manual of the Principles and Practice of Local Churches*, Gospel Trumpet Co., Anderson, IN, 1927, vi.

The Russell Byrum model of church governance does clearly reflect his belief in the leadership and authority of the lead pastor. He states: "[Pastoral] authority comes to him directly, however, from two sources and in that sense is of two kinds. (1) He receives authority directly from God. (2) He receives authority from God through the congregation and by their appointment. As the rule of Christ over men is not of the driving, compelling kind but rather a rule by love, so is the fundamental nature of the rule of the pastor. It is the power to influence God's people."[6]

But the system that Byrum introduced in his 1927 book (which still dominates Church of God practices) was a system based on the philosophy that there were two streams of work in the church: The spiritual work of discipleship; and the business work of the property and finances. His system calls for a number of boards and committees in each stream. In the spiritual stream the church is served by congregational elders and deacons. These two groups (elders and deacons) work with the pastor to oversee the religious education committee, the assistant pastor, the young people's leaders, the junior church leaders, and the Sunday school superintendent. Other Sunday school officers, department leaders, and teachers fall under the leadership of the Sunday school superintendent.

The business organization of the church is to be led by four standing committees: The board of trustees, five members who oversee the property of the church; a finance committee, consisting of three members who have charge of the collection and disbursing of the money of the church; a benevolence committee, consisting of three members, who distribute church funds to those in need; and a budget committee consisting of chairpersons of the previously mentioned committees and the officers of the congregation.

The bylaws suggested by Byrum are included as an addendum at the end of this book. You will see that provision is made for the appointment of additional committees as needed, as well as the description of a nominating committee of five persons.

In Byrum's system, the lead pastor is the ex-officio member of every board and every committee within the church. For over twenty years of my pastoral ministry, I served churches who utilized variations of the Russell Byrum bylaws. The existence of so many different decision-making groups led to a nightmare of scheduling complications as well as the gridlock and logjams in trying to coordinate decisions among committees.

6 Byrum, 94.

Understand Strategy, Tactics, and Logistics

Now that we've gained a historical perspective and understand how previous generations led our congregations toward a proliferation of boards and committees, let us further look at why church boards tend to get lost in logistics.

I want you to reflect on three terms, and the first is the word **strategy**. In this case, strategy is defined as the ultimate objective. In a war, for instance, the military would say that defeating the enemy is the strategy, or ultimate objective. In God's church we must be asking the Lord to keep our eyes on the ultimate objective which is to take back what hell has stolen.

The second word is **tactics**. In the military, tactics would describe the specific battles that must be won to achieve the ultimate objective or strategy.

To illustrate strategy and tactics, let's use an illustration from the days of World War II. The strategy to be achieved was world peace by the defeat of Japan and Germany. That was the ultimate objective. In the European theater, the strategy was to defeat Hitler and the German forces.

Since tactics describe the specific battles that must be won to achieve the strategic objective, a tactical plan was developed to combine the strength of the allied forces and break through the German stronghold at Normandy in France in a concentrated powerful sweep. It was believed that by breaking through the German fortifications, making their way across France, all the way to Berlin, victory could be achieved by demolishing the German headquarters. That was the tactical plan.

It is very interesting to read in historical documents about all that went into this Normandy invasion. The allied forces were under the command of the Supreme Allied Commander General Dwight D. Eisenhower.

The third word is **logistics**. In order to accomplish the Normandy invasion through successful concentrated efforts, the logistical needs of the allied forces had to be met. Tremendous logistical planning is involved in supplying the physical needs of the forces fighting the battle. Try to imagine some of the logistical needs. If you were to try to imagine them all, it would take reams of paper.

Popular Mechanics Magazine printed an August 1944 description of the logistical success of the D-Day Invasion:

> In speaking of the greatest military assault in history—the invasion

> of France by the Allied forces—Prime Minister Churchill said:
>
> "Everything proceeded according to plan. And what a plan!"
>
> The magnitude of that plan, worked out by persons Herr Hitler once called 'military idiots,' staggers the imagination. It embraced the air, ground and sea forces of this nation and our allies. It hurdled problems of supply and transport, of pre-invasion training, of production and improvement of weapons, of photo-reconnaissance and mapping on a scale that makes the battle plans of Napoleon look like a game of checkers. More than 125,000,000 maps alone, just to mention one item, were used in perfecting the master invasion plan.
>
> The success of that plan was demonstrated to a stunned enemy and a surprised world on D-Day. Four thousand ships carried the magnificently equipped troops across the English Channel under protection of a powerful naval force including 12 battleships, and thousands of aircraft.
>
> Parachute and airborne divisions, spearheading the invasion, filled the sky over Normandy. As a climax to the "combined operations" attack on German coastal defenses, Allied planes dropped 11,000 tons of bombs in the eight hours preceding the landing and big naval guns pounded the coast before the troops went ashore. In 10 minutes, 600 naval guns fired 2,000 tons of shells at Nazi batteries.[7]

We may be amazed at the answers to questions like: How many soldiers? How many tanks? What kind of munitions? How many bullets? How many aircraft carriers? How many planes and parachutes? How many ships? What about stretchers? What about latrine? What about medics? What were the rations for food? What about rope and ability to scale the cliffs? One can just begin to imagine all of the questions regarding logistics. But the people who were in leadership were not so much preoccupied with the logistics rather than the systems that were created that made the logistics work.

Do these three words make sense? The church leadership needs a clear **strategy**, the staff needs to be able to employ the **tactics**, and the members of the congregation work together to fulfill the **logistics**.

When it becomes clear in the church that the governing board helps the lead pastor to clarify the strategic objective, then the governing board can hold the pastor accountable for the fulfillment of the objective. I've learned

7 *How the D-Day Invasion Was Planned*, Popular Mechanics Magazine, August 1944.

from personal experience that tremendous progress is made when I have a board to whom I am accountable—and who keeps me accountable for ministry progress.

Earlier, when I described the needs of the children's ministry at Salem, we knew that one of the victories we needed was the leadership of a children's pastor. And so, we decided that we were going to channel church funds for the establishment of that role and that position on the payroll. The strategy was to win our community to Christ. The tactic was to add an effective children's pastor to the team. We went all out on this and it worked.

It became the children's ministry team, not the lead pastor or the board, that ultimately focused on the logistical needs of children's ministry. It became their job to supply the physical and organizational needs of the ministry volunteers.

Ministry growth occurs when the governance board is holding the lead pastor accountable to fulfill the objectives. What I've observed is that a lot of congregations get stalled because, at the board level, time is spent on logistical questions when the board should be dealing with the governance and the purpose questions.

An effective church board must systematically work towards eliminating all logistical items from the board meeting agenda. For example, the church board should not be discussing on its agenda whether or not they can approve the purchase of new tires for the church van. These logistical questions must be dealt with at other levels of the organization. There's another level of volunteer leadership of the church that needs to be dealing with that, but it's not the board's responsibility. To restate, if the board spends its time—its limited time—in logistical matters, then who gives direction to the overall ministry of the church to the community?

We have to make choices, and we have to set up systems in which we understand that there are different arenas of responsibility in the church.

We ask, who would have that responsibility? And then we begin to define roles more clearly. In our organization, we have this little team that looks after our property and we've empowered them. They have a budget. As that team does its work, they enjoy it. Actually, they love it; that's how God wired these people. Ministry becomes fun when God's people are released to do what He created them to do.

They love being involved in ministry, but they don't love going to meetings to get approval. Can you imagine trying to get approval to spend the money to replace the blades on the church-owned mower? Well, all in favor say aye. Come on. I'm being a little bit facetious, but not much. You must admit, I'm not too far off.

Let's set our church free by building our work around an understanding of strategy, tactics, and logistics. When we are clear about who needs to speak into each of those processes, life gets better!

Consider Why Church Boards Get Off-track So Easily

There's a simple answer to why church boards get off track. Simply said, we're not coming to the meeting alone. This illustration says that in this situation, seven families are attending the board meeting.

Influences from each person's family relationships

At the board table you see Susie, Carlos, Chris, Pat, Fred, Paula, and you. The small circles above their names represent all of the people who are speaking into their ears. Someone says, "The next time you go to the board, make sure you guys talk about x, y, and z."

At the board table it feels like each of the board members has many prompters speaking to them. When they feel obligated to bring small logistical concerns to the table, that's an ineffective way for the board to work. In those instances, the governing work of the board is distracted away from the strategy or tactics they need to discuss.

Imagine if the board member named Fred comes to the board meeting and says, "When are we going to paint the stalls in the ladies' room?" You have a pretty safe conclusion that Fred hasn't been hanging out in the ladies' room! He's speaking on behalf of someone else who expects the board to be concerned with small logistical matters. There is a better way!

In the following pages you will see that the formation of one single governance board that oversees and gives accountability to the work of the lead pastor is the healthier way. Ministries of the church that once were led by committees, voting and preparing minutes, now are led by ministry team leaders. The orientation is no longer toward a legislative approach to ministry, but a discipleship and multiplication orientation. Read on to chapter three, "Planning for a Better Way," and continue on this journey toward a healthy decision-making structure in your church.

CHAPTER 3

Planning for a Better Way

Many important lessons are learned through decades of ministry. Among the most important is this: Avoid making abrupt leadership moves or announcing major changes without allowing congregants to speak into the process. Thus, your recommendation for changes to the church governance and decision-making system should be made patiently over time. Most thoughtful church members deeply desire to see their church function in a healthy manner with solid decisions being made in the absence of conflict and drama. The following steps will help to ensure a peaceful path of change paved with careful planning.

Review existing bylaws and identify ways they limit and/or empower forward motion

What's the advantage of this governance system and how is it created? When a board governs, its relationship to the ministry is quite different than when the board manages. This is probably the biggest point of all. I'm recommending that you think about your congregation's future in terms of a board that works with pastoral leadership to imagine the future, and to hold the pastor accountable to lead in a way in which that vision is fulfilled.

There are crucial ways that a governing board is quite different than a managing board. Most of the congregations I have encountered have managing boards, but no one really governs the strategic objectives of the ministry—no one really visions. As a result, most churches in North America are small. A full two-thirds of all of the congregations in the church group I belong to have less than 80 people attending on Sunday morning. Statistics show this is common with other church groups as well.

I am convinced that a major limiting factor keeping churches small is a systemic problem—or a problem with the leadership system. It's the way we think about how decisions get made that holds churches back.

When our church staff was under the management board system, we used to laugh about how things never seemed to break until the day after Tuesday's board of trustees meeting. At that point you knew you were going to struggle along with it for a month until the board met again and gave permission to spend the money to fix it. What a slow and frustrating way to operate! Of course, in an emergency, we were able to navigate a way to get a repair made, but there were many other instances when important approval had to wait for a month. This describes the frustration when the day-to-day management is being done by the board rather than by a governance system that empowers staff to manage.

Continue to educate yourselves on a new model

The system of decision making I'm describing lifts the one governing board of the congregation to their rightful place of spiritual leadership within the body of Christ. Members are chosen by spiritual qualifications, not by vocational backgrounds, nor as representatives of another committee in the church. In his insightful work *Transforming Church Boards into Communities*, author Charles M. Olsen writes:

> To apply Paul's word to those who serve on boards and councils is simply to extend the principle. The council is not a second-class citizen or an advisory voice to the ears of power. Laypeople are empowered by virtue of their baptism, gifts, and calling by the Spirit. The voice of the congregation has set them apart by installation (or in some cases ordination) to do a work of ministry called leadership. They are not representatives of special groups or interests in the church. They are set apart to seek God's will for the church and its ministry in the world. What's more, the ethos or character of the congregation is manifest in the composition of the council, lending it great authority to get things done. What empowerment![8]

The illustration on the next page helps to describe this simple, practical, and effective means of decision making.

The largest oval at the top represents the congregation, consisting of a certain number of individuals that make up the business association of the church. From among their ranks is a smaller circle which represents the governing board. Notice that this group is pictured as a smaller subset of the larger congregation. The church body has designated these individuals to represent the interest of the congregation and believes these are spiritually qualified people who will work alongside the lead pastor to achieve the strategic objective of the ministry, and to envision the future of the church.

8 Charles M. Olsen, *Transforming Church Boards into Communities of Spiritual Leaders* (10). Rowman & Littlefield Publishers, 1995. Kindle Edition, 2014.

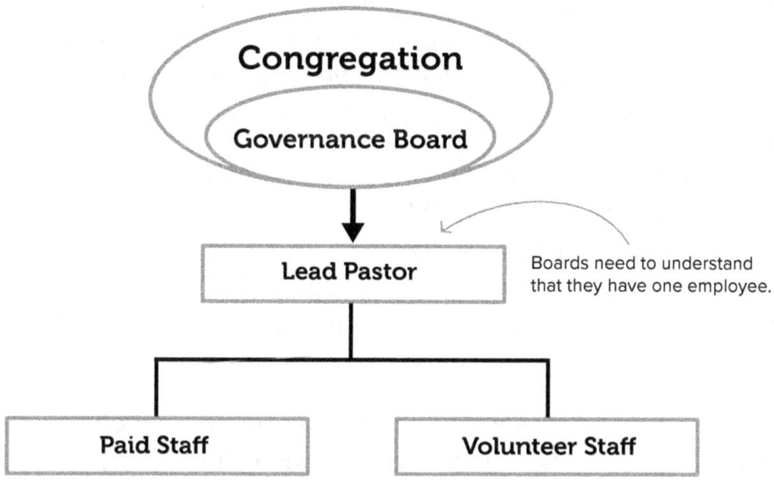

Next the board needs to understand that in principle, they have one employee and it's their lead pastor. The lead pastor is accountable to the board, and the paid staff and volunteer staff are accountable to the lead pastor.

Consider the rationale for quarterly board meetings

In over forty years of ministry, I have had the opportunity to serve on the board of trustees of a small Christian college, on the board of our national church's pension and retirement investment firm, and for two terms as chairman of our national church general assembly and ministry council, overseeing the work of our national executive. In each of those experiences where millions of dollars were being managed, the board met on a periodic basis, two to three times each year.

In none of those boards were we involved in the day-to-day management decisions. We weren't involved in decisions about whether or not a new maintenance person was hired to run the campus, nor were we even involved in the decisions of hiring professors. We were involved in the overall direction of the college. We were the governing board. This is the principle that I introduced to local churches I served as pastor. When our boards began to meet quarterly instead of monthly, life got better for everyone. Our agenda was populated by the big-picture view of the ministry, our outreach to the community, and the overall financial and spiritual health of the congregation.

We noticed that having a quarterly financial review gave much better perspective than a month-by-month view. Trends in giving were easier to recognize when the board had a longer and higher overview.

As we began meeting on a quarterly basis, I was able to present the governing board with a lead pastor's quarterly report at each meeting. The report would be anywhere from twelve to twenty pages long, single-spaced. It gave an overview of each of the ministries of the church.

Board members recognized that they had a better view of the ministry than they previously did in the monthly meetings. An additional benefit of the thorough quarterly reports was the ease in consolidating information from three quarterly reports into an annual report. The annual report became a compilation of the highlights of the quarterly reports, and suddenly life got better and simpler for many of the church leaders.

In another important observation of the organizational chart, you'll notice that under the lead pastor are paid staff and volunteer staff. In this system there is a new definition of staff. In this definition of staff, there are some people who are empowered to function as staff even though they're not on the payroll, and they volunteer their time and service.

My mom, as a director of Christian education, operated that way in my home church. She met on a periodic basis with the pastoral staff to plan and develop the educational ministry of the church. Even though she was never paid, she was considered a staff person—a volunteer staff in the local church. There can be a number of other ways you could consider people in the church who could meet with the paid staff for the planning and the operation of the ministries of the church. When volunteer staff meet to plan ministry in cooperation with the paid staff team, the dynamics are much different. The meetings are more professional, outcomes are clearer, and the group functions much differently than a traditional committee. When paid and volunteer staff assemble to minister together in Jesus' name, the group functions more like a ministry team and not like a committee creating minutes and passing motions.

Here is a hypothetical illustration of a volunteer staff position: Imagine a local congregation has a five-acre property. Imagine there's a fellow in the congregation who used to be the head of maintenance at the local school district, and now he's retired. He receives a pension and has adequate retirement income, but he's bored. His wife wants him out of the house, and he likes doing the things he used to do as the head of maintenance at the school. So, he comes over to the church and says, "Hey guys, I will take on the responsibility for maintenance here, acting as head of the maintenance team. I don't need to be on the payroll. Just put me to work."

This sounds like a dream come true! What church wouldn't love to be the recipient of the efforts of such a person? Imagine putting this man in the position of a volunteer staff person in charge of the maintenance. Imagine that he was also willing to organize other volunteers for the mowing and maintenance schedule.

When we served at Salem Church, the campus was 65 acres. We had pretty big equipment, and we had a whole team of people that had their own mowing schedule. A volunteer team took care of mowing, trimming and landscaping. Flowers were planted. Weeds were pulled. I mean, that place was manicured, because these people love trimming bushes, spreading mulch, and making the place look great. It was all done on a volunteer basis, but we still had a staff person who was overseeing this kind of stuff.

We had paid persons and we also had volunteer people who were given appropriate empowerment, so that if they needed to have the mower blades replaced, and it was going to cost money, there was a budget. They could just submit those bills to the office, and they would be paid. They were empowered to be good managers, and they were trusted.

A new sense of joy, purpose, and professionalism emerges in the church when the board begins to govern instead of manage and when paid and volunteer staff are empowered and respected. Great things happen when good people are empowered to make wise decisions. I must admit that in the former way of doing things, replete with many boards and committees, I sometimes felt like half of the people were given steering wheels and the other half were given brake pedals. On the old "committee bus" it was all too seldom that anyone stepped on the gas!

Another important principle in the governance board system is that the board has no authority to circumvent the lead pastor and take on a supervisory role with staff members. By bypassing the authority of the board's one employee (the lead pastor), staff members will begin to believe that they need not please their boss. They only need to please the board.

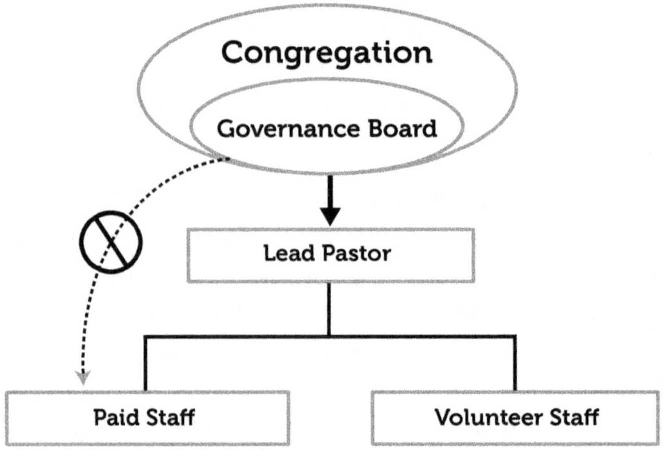

Note: The Church Board may not "go around" the lead pastor to give instructions to the staff. This usurps authority.

When the board goes around the lead pastor to give instructions, supervision, or review to the staff team members, they are usurping the authority of the person they've put in charge of the staff. This is one of the most important rules that must be diligently followed. To violate this principle is to create a very dysfunctional situation.

Remember one important word that is the hinge upon which this system turns. The word is **clarity**. When we get clear about who makes decisions and why they make certain decisions, then we have health in the local church. This is the foundation of a healthy decision-making structure. So, at the Salem church, we often referred to three words: leadership, management, and governance. The two preceding organizational charts reflect the board's relationship to the organization in the decision-making structure. The pastor is the interlocutor between the board and staff. The board worked in cooperation with the pastor and did not go around the pastor to give instructions directly to the staff.

In his excellent book, *Winning on Purpose*, John Edmund Kaiser provides a chart that clearly describes the different leadership roles in the church. In describing the chart on the next page, he says, "The connection of mission to action is represented by noting that the board articulates mission, the pastor translates the mission into vision (a picture of mission-accomplished within a specific context and period), and the staff translates the vision into action."[9]

9 Dr. John E. Kaiser, Thomas G. Bandy, Bill Easum. *Winning on Purpose: How to Organize Congregations to Succeed in Their Mission* (Convergence EBook Series) (Kindle Locations 2101-2103). Abingdon Press. Kindle Edition, 2010.

MANAGEMENT	LEADERSHIP	GOVERNANCE
Is entrusted to the staff	Is entrusted to the lead pastor	Is entrusted to the board
Executes with excellence	Directs with excellence	Protects with excellence
Does things right	Does the right things	Defines what is right
Contributes efficiency	Contributes effectiveness	Contributes accountability
Answers to the lead pastor	Answers to the board	Answers to the church
Translates vision to action	Translates purpose to vision	Articulates purpose
Links pastor to ministries	Links staff to board	Links board to congregation
Operates within boundaries	Enforces boundaries	Establishes boundaries
Runs tactical operations	Runs strategic operations	Writes and monitors policy
Meets frequently	Meets with staff and the board	Meets infrequently
Solves problems of today	Solves problems of tomorrow	Prioritizes the problems

From *Winning on Purpose* by John Kaiser

The new structure articulates the purpose and links the board to the congregation. The board establishes boundaries and writes and monitors policy. That's a really, really important function. The board meets infrequently—in quarterly meetings where it prioritizes the problems. For example, the Salem board helped me to identify three critical success factors; together, we identified which challenge we should address first. It was the children's ministry. Next was youth ministry and the third was small group ministry. We went after all of them, and by solving all of those the church moved forward. But the board was really helpful, because they were helping me to clarify.

In one of our board retreats, we identified ten things that needed to be done that were critical success factors for the future of the church—ten things loomed before us. But we knew we couldn't address all ten at the same time. It's like that illustration of the man who jumps on his horse and rides off in every direction. You can't do that. You can only ride off in one direction. And so, the governing board gave wise advice in setting the priority of children's ministry first, youth ministry second, and small group ministry third. We realized that if those ministries floundered it would compromise the ability of the congregation to transform lives of people in the community who were without Christ.

We addressed those in a cascading sense of priorities. And as we gave attention to those things, the benefits, or the blessings in the church, were measurable. We saw the results of these priorities because we knew what we needed to do to reach the community.

In one presentation I made on this subject, I was asked to define the phrase found in the chart, "Governance—Protects with excellence." I described the protection offered by the governing board in two ways. First, the governing board protects the leader (the lead pastor, CEO). The leader who is on point gets the arrows shot at him, and the board protects the leader. Why? Because the board is governing the leader, and the leader is not doing anything the board doesn't know about.

Secondly, it also protects the organization from the leader. The governing board protects the principles by which the organization is governed. This means that the leader is accountable to the board and does not have permission to lead outside the boundaries the board has established. This is important as it relates to how people and financial resources are treated.

It may sound confusing to think that the governing board protects the organization from the leader. I remember a very effective concept from my time with the Carver Governance training in Atlanta a few years ago that can help to clarify this principle.

If you have a horse, you probably have a pasture connected to your barn. The horse can go inside the barn if it's raining or the horse can, if the door's open, go out into the pasture and graze. And you probably don't care where the horse goes in the pasture, as long as the horse stays inside the fence.

If you felt like the horse needed a bigger pasture, you'd make a bigger fence. There also may be reasons that you would tighten the fence and make the pasture smaller. You are mainly concerned with the horse staying in the pasture. Governance is what sets the boundaries for the leader of an organization—similar to the fences surrounding a pasture.

If you prefer a sports analogy, whether it's a basketball court or a football field, there are boundaries the player may not step across or the whistle blows. It means the player stepped out of bounds. This is what is meant when we say the governing board protects with excellence. It sets the boundaries and limitations for their one employee's leadership parameters.

In the places I've led with this system, my delegated staff and I knew how much authority we had to spend church funds due to the language of the bylaws and the policies of the board. Our latitude was limited by the rules. In the church the lead pastor's latitude depends on what the board feels is the appropriate level of trust. It is also a reflection on the amount of trust gained by the lead pastor.

You can make the boundaries as tight or as broad as you feel serves the purposes of the church. That's what protecting with excellence means. For instance, the governing board protects the church from the leader by saying they don't want a leader to overspend the funds of the church and put the church into a deficit position; therefore, the board makes a rule that protects the church from the leader.

On the other hand, when you're protecting the leader from the church, you're protecting the leader from taking all the arrows because you're clarifying reality for the congregation. You remind constituents, the board made certain decisions that reflect exactly what leadership decided they were going to do and they're doing it together.

Create subcommittees of the governing board for verification

An important aspect of governing is verification. Quarterly ministry and financial reports are given to the governing board, yet without verification or testing, the board is not governing most effectively. The old adage, "Trust but verify," comes into play here. You must be able to verify what is true. A subcommittee of the governing board can serve as a financial audit committee to verify," that the reports submitted are accurate. This same committee can interview and retain a financial accounting firm, which provides consultation and review of the church's procedures and records. Due to the expense of a full audit, I recommend that an audit be conducted every third year and a review of the books by an accounting firm be done in the intervening years.

In similar manner, a personnel subcommittee can be appointed to consult with the lead pastor in decisions where he or she may ask for input. It is also important for the subcommittee to check with staff to ensure that regularly scheduled, periodic staff reviews are taking place, as well as to verify that the workplace environment is positive and encouraging.

These important subcommittees demonstrate that the governing board always has the ability to reach as deeply as needed into the organizational systems to ensure that what is being reported to the board is verified as accurate and true.

Create an atmosphere of collaboration

In his book, *Free to Lead*, Rod Stafford introduces a third way of organizational decision making. He calls it a collaborative hierarchy.

> Simply stated, collaborative hierarchy provides clarity concerning the ultimate ownership of a decision based on positional authority within the hierarchy but encourages the decision maker to invite others into the conversation, regardless of position in the hierarchy, for the purpose of making the best decision possible. In a collaborative hierarchy, positional authority is most profoundly demonstrated in the freedom of the decision maker to determine who is brought into the conversation.[10]

I experienced the power of a collaborative hierarchy in leading the staff teams in both the Michigan and Ohio congregations. When the staff was assembled, I knew they possessed valuable insights and perspectives from their particular vantage point in the organization. There were times, for instance, when I needed the perspective of our receptionist in considering certain decisions. When people walked into the church office on weekdays and were looking for somebody or bringing a delivery, our receptionist was the person to greet them. Therefore, there were times when I sought out the perspective of the receptionist in a staff meeting since she was the initial contact person with a walk-in visitor or with a phone call.

Sometimes our receptionist would identify a potential problem and offer a new solution. Consequently, she felt empowered to speak and was respected by others when she shared her opinion. The same principle applied to other staff input sought on various proposed changes and schedule alterations.

In a collaborative hierarchy the lead pastor has the authority to overrule the preferences or recommendations of the staff team, yet wisdom demonstrates the value of listening to the voices of others. The point is, the staff team has some observations that will help the lead pastor make better decisions.

The organizational structure gives the lead pastor the authority to make the decisions, but this system encourages the decision maker to call others to speak into the decision. This is demonstrated when the lead pastor asks the staff team for input. You would observe active listening happening. The

10 Rod Stafford, *Free to Lead: The Decision-making Ethos of Healthy Growing Churches*, published in Fairfax, VA by Rod Stafford, 2011, 5-6.

leader nods his or her head and gains insights and understanding. Then, the lead pastor says, "That's interesting. Okay, tell me more," and keeps asking questions. Information is being gleaned from different people in the room. Finally, he or she would say, "Wow, thank you everyone for your input. That really helps me make a better decision." That's the description of a collaborative hierarchy at work, which functions in stark contrast to a dictatorship or an autocratic rule.

In a collaborative hierarchy, the lead pastor delegates a good number of decisions and responsibilities to others within the staff or the organization, but ultimate accountability for those decisions remains with the lead pastor. The system works well when strong trust exists in both directions, from the one who delegates—and from the one who carries out the assignment. In this instance, the one who has an assignment feels empowered to make decisions regarding the implementation of the task assigned, meaning that the one entrusted with a task or responsibility does not need to continually check back with the lead pastor or receive permission at every turn.

A collaborative atmosphere presupposes that empowerment is given. So, if an administrative assistant is given the responsibility of keeping office supplies stocked, and writing tablets are running low, no permission is needed to place an order. The employee is trusted to accomplish the task and fulfill the needs of the office. In this instance, she was more responsible for the result than she was the process. If the process is regulated too tightly, she can't keep the supplies stocked if the pastor's gone and no one is available to give permission to order what is needed.

The next sentence in the Stafford quote says, "In a collaborative hierarchy, positional authority is most profoundly demonstrated in the freedom of the decision maker to determine who is brought into the conversation."[11]

Not everyone's time needs to be consumed in considering every decision. The right people are brought into the conversation at appropriate times. Usually, people are more supportive of decisions when they've been involved in the discussion.

Two words should constantly be reviewed in a collaborative hierarchy—**decisions** and **discussion**. It's important to create an atmosphere for open discussion where opinions are sought and heard. Ultimately, the lead pastor will make a decision based on the discussion that has ensued. The result is a wise decision, taking many factors into account, and a team that

11 Stafford.

feels respected and heard. This does not mean, however, that each person on a staff team will heartily agree with each decision. They will most likely respect the decision and the rationale behind it since an honest attempt at broad input was demonstrated by the leader.

This behavior builds great credibility in the organization. In the two pastorates where this model was adopted, another interesting reality developed in congregational life. As we went to this system of clearly defined decision making, our business meetings became less contentious, and trust levels increased greatly because people felt we had clearly defined systems for making decisions and that appropriate discussions happened before decisions were made.

Announce decisions and build trust systematically

A crucial aspect of healthy decision making is healthy decision communication. This is where many leaders underestimate the value of a systematic approach to communication. I confess that I learned this lesson the hard way. Early in my pastorate in Michigan, with three full-time and one part-time associate pastors, I made the unfortunate mistake of announcing a ministry decision from the pulpit in a Sunday service. When I felt an iciness in the staff meeting that week, I finally coaxed out of the team their frustration. They told me they were caught offguard and taken by surprise with the announcement. They told me it was an unfair way to lead, and they pointed out, kindly but firmly, that they felt I had overstepped my bounds. I had breached an unwritten protocol—the associate pastors were hearing about a new direction that had never been discussed with them prior to the Sunday announcement.

I owned it, admitted my error, and empathized with their feelings. "I know that must've felt really awkward, and I promise I'll never do that again," I said. But a promise is only good when you have a way to avoid doing the same thing again. So, I developed this system that I've used in ministry for the last 25 years. The illustration on the next page describes the systematic communication system I employed as a pastor. Like dropping a pebble in a pond, you see the outward ripples of communication.

In the collaborative discussion there may have been many voices, but when the decision is made, it needs to be systematically communicated, whether it's an idea or the discussion of a new ministry initiative.

Standard Sequence of Communication

This refers to ministry decisions that need to be communicated widely.

Note: Skipping any of these steps causes stress, confusion, and misunderstandings.

By the time it is announced to the congregation, the staff and ministry leaders have been made fully aware and are most likely on board. This healthy system is like propelling a rocket. It may look like a slow launch, but speed is quickly built.

When trust is built and people feel included in decision making and in the communication of plans, a sense of health and momentum emerges that brings great joy to all. This is the better way!

Construct a new decision-making model

It's important that pastors continue to educate themselves in the governance model of healthy decision making. Many resources are available in the library, on the internet, and through booksellers. The purpose of this book is to give you an introduction to these concepts as well as to suggest step-by-step methods of implementing the governance system in your church.

So far, I have described many reasons that pastors and church leaders are frustrated, confused and bogged down. I've introduced ideas to create understanding of a new way of thinking and making decisions. But I'm strongly recommending that you do not try to "go it alone" or build a new system for your congregation without consulting others. I would recommend you seek a coach to guide your church through the process. The coach doesn't have authority over your ministry so much as he or she asks questions and helps you stay on track with your process. The coach can be a key voice in helping you gain congregational buy-in to a restructuring of the church's decision-making process.

I strongly encourage you to adopt a model set of bylaws as the foundation upon which your new structure can be built. Appendix 2 at the end of this book provides the basic structure by which the First Church of God in St. Joseph, Michigan is governed, as well as the Salem Church of God in Clayton, Ohio. These bylaws were originally created by Rod Stafford in Fairfax, Virginia and were used for many years at the Fairfax Community Church. They have been only slightly altered.

Many churches desire to incorporate official policy statements as a part of their bylaws. I caution against inserting policy statements into a governance document. I would recommend that these be added at the back of the bylaws as official policies adopted by the congregation. These could include the Scriptural and spiritual qualifications of leadership, statements on social issues that churches now are facing (such as a stance on marriage), and the policy about what types of ceremonies can be conducted on the church property or in the church facilities. These could be identified as operational policies. I highly recommend these types of policies be scrutinized by your attorney prior to adoption.

Bylaws will provide clarity on the decisions to be made by the entire congregation. The sample bylaws included in Appendix 2 list these decisions as:

1. Call of a senior pastor
2. Purchase or sale of real property or buildings
3. Incurring of long-term debt
4. Approval of the annual general operating budget
5. Individual ratification of governing board members
6. Alteration, amendment or repeal of the constitution & bylaws

The bylaws will also give clarity on certain decisions to be made by the governing board as well as decisions that are the responsibility of the lead pastor. This clarity is important beyond measure. When the congregation is confused about who makes what decision, conflict is certain to develop. In the midst of confusion, people will ask, "Who gave them the right to make that decision?"

Consider the importance of legal review

The creation of church bylaws is not entirely a do-it-yourself project. It is imperative that the proposed bylaws undergo legal review. To the best of my knowledge, I believe that in most states the articles of incorporation on file with the state take precedence over the bylaws as the defining legal document of the congregation. The articles of incorporation and the bylaws are different documents that serve different purposes, but they need to be in harmony with each other. This is yet another reason that legal counsel should be sought.

What's included in church bylaws?

The *Model Nonprofit Corporations Act (3rd ed. 2008)* also states that:

> The bylaws of a nonprofit corporation may contain any provision for managing the activities and regulating the affairs of the corporation that is not inconsistent with law or the articles of incorporation. The following subjects generally pertain to managing the activities and regulating the affairs of a church, and are commonly included in a church's bylaws:
>
> - Qualifications, selection, and expulsion of members
> - Time and place of annual business meetings
> - The calling of special business meetings
> - Notice for annual and special meetings
> - Quorums at meetings of the membership and church board
> - Voting rights and requirements
> - Selection, tenure, and removal of officers and directors
> - Filling of vacancies on the church board
> - Responsibilities of directors and officers
> - The procedure for amending bylaws
> - The procedure and voting requirements for purchases and conveyances of church property
>
> The designation of standing committees (such as an audit committee, an investment committee, and an insurance committee)

> The drafting of church bylaws is a complex task that should not be attempted without the assistance of an attorney. Knowing what to include and exclude from your bylaws are important tasks that require legal knowledge and experience.[12]

Review the size of the governing board and nonresident board members

In the sample bylaws presented in Appendix 2 of this book you will read:

Section 2.1 - GOVERNING BOARD MEMBERSHIP - The Governing Board shall be composed of not less than nine or more than twelve members individually ratified by the Corporation, plus the Senior Pastor, who is an exofficio, nonvoting member. Two members of the Governing Board shall be chosen from outside of the Corporation. Both shall be recognized leaders in the Church of God, Anderson, IN.

Take the opportunity to develop next-generation leaders for the church

The membership of the governing board is described as "not less than nine or more than twelve." Some may wonder why this range of participation was created. At first, we created this range in order to allow for the number of spiritual leaders the nominating committee and the governing board believed God had raised up in the body. If, for example, it was believed that the Lord had raised up twelve spiritually gifted people to serve on the governing board, the bylaws provided for that; however, if it seemed there were only nine or ten who had those gifts, the bylaws allowed for that too. Later, we came to realize that the range of numbers provided us with an opportunity to ratify some younger, next-generation leaders to serve on the governing board. That is what we did at the Salem Church, and the results of that decision have blessed the church greatly!

As you begin to plan for the governance board path of healthy decision making in your church, I strongly recommend you create a pathway for next-generation leaders to sit in the governing circle alongside the more seasoned leaders. When you read the Scriptural qualifications of leadership in 1 Timothy, verse 6 cautions, *He must not be a recent convert, or he may become conceited and fall under the same judgment as the devil.* This is a good reminder to us that we should seek individuals who, although younger in chronological years, are not recent converts or as the New King James states it, *novices in the faith*.

12 Richard Hammar, *What You Need to Know About Church Bylaws*, adapted from "Governing Well," Church Law & Tax Report, 2015. Online at www.ChurchLawAndTax.com.

Benefit from the nonresident board members' wisdom

One of the greatest benefits to this governance system is the ability of the church to tap the wisdom of leaders from outside the local body. At first, this was a difficult concept to communicate to the congregational leaders for two primary reasons. First, it was a completely new and never-before-considered concept. Second, in the mindset of a management board mentality, they wondered whether or not nonresident board members would have the necessary perspective of the local needs and situation. I'm happy to say that in both of my former pastorates, the congregations not only embraced this concept, but have come to cherish the participation of the nonresident governing board members and the insights they bring to the table.

The fact that these nonresident board members are not limited by looking at matters completely through a "local lens" or perspective is best seen when a personnel situation or any other relational quandary comes to the board's attention. While local board members tend to look at the situation by considering the **personalities** of those involved, the nonresident board members look at the situation in light of the **principles** that come into play.

Since the nonresident board members don't know the persons involved in a situation, their perspective is broader. The resident board members are more likely to be cognizant of the political implications within the church body, so both perspectives are needed. Both viewpoints are important, but many times the lens of personalities involved overpower the principles that need to be viewed. If there is misbehavior going on in the congregation and the board knows it really needs to be dealt with, but hesitate, knowing that someone's relative is going to have a fit, the best decisions might be overruled by a desire to avoid that conflict. Nonresident board members tend to help the group embrace the higher view and do the right thing.

Another viewpoint the nonresident board members bring to the table is a perspective that will help the board to think in ways they might not otherwise consider, expanding on what might be a limited, local perspective.

I began to see the value of nonresident members as I served on several different boards in national ministries of the Church of God movement. My work on a college board, as well as the Board of Pensions, the Division of World Service, and as chair of the Church of God Ministries Council convinced me that having board members with wide-ranging perspectives was very beneficial. People from across the nation are assembled in forming boards to govern these national ministries.

Just as our national ministries are well-served by members who come from Philadelphia, Orlando, Houston, or Los Angeles, so our churches are well-served when we have people from outside our local congregation sit at the table. A board is particularly well-served by its non-resident members during a pastoral transition. I believe both the St. Joseph church and the Salem church had a much better pastoral transition when I resigned due to the wisdom of nonresident board members who provided reassuring perspective to the board.

The presence of the outside board members was not only a stabilizing force, giving perspective at my departure, but they also were very helpful in the search process. Potential pastoral candidates knew they could call the nonresident board members for an objective perspective in considering an invitation from the search committee.

The late Dr. Gilbert Stafford, a great theology professor at Anderson (IN) School of Theology, pointed out that when a church preaches enthusiastically about Christian unity, it is certainly odd to see congregations of that group operate in isolation. To welcome nonresident board members is to embrace interdependent relationships that reflect autonomy and foster accountability.

I have personally participated in this interdependent system for twenty years within the Church of God, and I've found it to be effective and enriching for all involved. I'm grateful to see more and more congregations adopting the discipline of inviting notable leaders to their board tables.

It's interesting to see how those who are respected leaders within the larger church, who have demonstrated a capacity to think some big thoughts, are happy to make themselves available to help other churches in God's Kingdom work. I believe the inclusion of nonresident board members is one of the most positive trends happening within the church family across North America.

CHAPTER 4

Communicating the Need for Change

Now let's consider communication of the governance system to the congregation. Once leaders begin planning the look of the new structure and fine-tuning it, the very important task of communicating with the congregation remains.

There are five steps to communicating the governance plan to the church:

1. Introduce the rationale for change
2. Give adequate lead time for people to process and think
3. Share initial thoughts and plans across church leadership base
4. Conduct information meetings to answer questions and address concerns
5. Announce the date for a congregational decision

The timeline and patience needed in the process will vary from congregation to congregation. In a newly formed congregation, for example, there is little need to reassure members of the wisdom of changing long-standing traditions in decision making. I had to navigate these changes in two congregations that had been around for a century. In this case, I really had to build the rationale. Why would we want to change? We've been doing it this way for 100 years! So I had to really tune up my message. I explained that in the way we were functioning, we were wearing out the people.

Step one:

Introduce the rationale for change to the church

The phrase, wearing out the people, hearkens to Exodus, chapter 18, when Jethro, Moses' father-in-law, said to him, "You're wearing out yourself but you're also wearing out the people in the way you're making decisions." In each of those churches people were tired of going to committee meetings, and this was our foundation as we began to introduce a rationale for change.

I began explaining to congregational leaders that a ministry team functions very differently from a committee. I reminded them that the bylaws limited the number of people who could serve and prescribed that the committee must meet on a monthly basis. I helped them see that the limitation set on the number of committee members artificially capped participation in the ministry. In contrast, a ministry team consisted of all those who had a passion for or interest in a particular ministry. The team did not meet in a legislative session with minutes, reports, and voting. Instead, the team met to huddle together, plan ministry, and enjoy the work they were doing together. The change of approach was refreshing to many.

The ministry team for vacation Bible school provided a great example. They met a lot in the weeks preceding VBS. But they didn't meet very much in the couple of months after VBS. There was an ebb and flow to their work. They met as the need presented itself. This helped people begin to see the flexibility of a ministry team approach.

Step two:
Give adequate lead time for people to process and think

Once the rationale for a governance system is presented, it's important to give adequate lead time for people to process and think. Other leaders in the organization will help to carry the idea forward and ease anxieties that some church members may express.

Again, this slow and steady approach is more applicable to changing a long-standing system in an older church body than it is for younger or newly organized congregations. The lead time in younger, more agile congregations may be shorter than for those churches that are making a change from long-standing bylaws in a tradition-bound setting.

Step three:
Share initial thoughts and plans across church leadership base

It is beneficial to begin openly discussing the exploration of a new decision-making model. This helps the congregation to be prepared for coming changes. The many conversations that ensue are all helpful in building an atmosphere of openness and trust. By sharing initial thoughts and plans openly in the church, it lessens or even eliminates the perception that a group is planning to ramrod a new idea forward in spite of the church's wishes.

One example of new thinking that needs to be embraced is the redefinition of staff to include paid staff and volunteer staff. This is a new concept for most people, yet when given time to think about it, the idea makes a lot of sense to them.

Author John Kaiser says,

> *Winning on Purpose* uses the term staff in a comprehensive and functional manner. Staff includes full-time, part-time, and unpaid ministry managers that head up every major team or department throughout the organization. Areas traditionally viewed as "spiritual," such as worship and education, are included, but so are areas that are traditionally viewed as "practical," such as facilities and finances. So, the term staff is comprehensive not only with regard to categories of employment, but also with regard to categories of activity. Each of the two kinds of categories raises a question. Why refer to unpaid leaders of major ministries as staff? Because the responsibility, authority, and accountability attached to this level of management are the same regardless of employment factors. So-called "volunteers" managing a division of ministry are, in fact, compensated according to their effectiveness in an accountable leadership setting, even though compensation in the form of appreciation and fulfillment is intangible. And so-called "professionals" doing the same job are motivated by those same intangibles, in addition to their wages. Finally, the use of the word staff makes it easy to perceive and remember that the top ministry coordinators work as part of the pastor's team. In the United States at least, staff readily connotes a team directed by a primary leader.[13]

This elevation of important ministry leaders as a part of the staff raises the overall sense of professionalism and seriousness by which ministry is considered. Forward motion in ministry is enhanced due to the sense of empowerment and partnership that is given.

Step four:
Conduct information meetings to answer questions and address concerns

It may come as a surprise to pastors and church leaders how deeply congregants care about how the decision-making structure of their congregation is organized. After all, most of the time when the church body gathers, bylaws and church governance are not conversations that rise to the forefront. My discovery, however, was that people had keen interest in the subject of governance, and it was very worthwhile to create a forum for questions, answers and discussion. In both churches where new bylaws were implemented, we received some very good input in the information

13 Kaiser, *Winning*, Kindle 2114-2125.

meetings, which allowed for some tweaks and adjustments to the proposed bylaws. It also fostered the idea that the process of accepting a new system was collaborative and inclusive.

Print the proposed bylaws and make them available for people to pick up, take home, and read. The front page should be clearly labeled, "Proposed Bylaws" or "Sample Bylaws" to indicate that they are a work in process and awaiting congregational input.

We scheduled a series of information meetings at various times in order to accommodate the typical busy schedules of our congregants. For instance, we had information meetings announced for Saturday afternoon, Sunday evening, Monday evening, and Wednesday evening (in the midst of the regular Wednesday evening activities). The many options further communicated to the congregation that every attempt was made to conduct an open and informative process in introducing a new governance structure.

In one congregation an individual who was part of a legacy family in the church was very anxious and somewhat agitated regarding the proposed change to the bylaws and governance structure. My description of a legacy family is one that has been a part of the congregation for multiple generations. He attended one of the information meetings with a prepared list of questions. It just so happened that he was the only congregant who attended this particular information meeting. There were three of us seated together at the table. An associate pastor, this gentleman, and me. He pulled a folded sheet of paper from his shirt pocket and unfolded it briskly.

I could tell there was some angst in him as he said, "I have a lot of questions."

"Great, I'm so glad you came prepared. That means a lot," I responded. "This means we'll have a productive conversation."

He started going down through the questions. Number one, I answered thoroughly. Number two, I answered the question, and so we continued.

By the time we got all the way through that sheet of paper, he flipped the sheet over. And I don't know what was printed on the other side, but all of a sudden, he started folding up that paper, put it back in his pocket, and said, "Pastor, you have sufficiently answered all my questions. You have my full support!"

Interactions like that proved to me the value of an information meeting. Taking an open and nondefensive approach that demonstrates a willingness to answer questions, creates big-time buy-in from the congregation.

There is one additional interaction with the man from the legacy family that I should share. I returned to visit my former congregation a few years after I left that pastorate. This same man came to me, gave me a big hug, and said, "Thank you, pastor, for everything you did to implement a new way forward for this church."

And I thought, *Well, this is interesting*. When he came into that meeting all those years ago, I felt like he was coming in as an antagonist, and now, he's really become an ally. And so, to me that showed the beauty of making sure that you have buy-in, that people's questions are answered, and that nobody feels like we're shoving something down their throat.

One of the most important things in leading a congregation is to demonstrate an openness to answering questions, listening to input, and eliminating fears with helpful reassurance. This, as much as anything else, endears a pastoral leader to a congregation.

When people feel church decisions offer an open process and their questions or concerns are heard, that's a big trust builder. As a leader I've always found it helpful to imagine I was on the other side of the table. How would I want change to be announced? How would I like for my questions to be answered?

Step five:
Announce the date for a congregational decision

When making the proposed bylaws available and announcing the scheduled time for the informational meetings, it's important to announce the date of the congregational business meeting at the same time. I recommend the meeting be announced about sixty to ninety days in advance. To announce a business meeting to adopt new bylaws only one or two weeks in advance can be an anxiety-producing announcement. It contributes the feeling of a hurried approach that eliminates the opportunity for due process. While not all church matters can afford to be dealt with over such a long span of time, it is beneficial to the health of the church in the long run to introduce something as big as a governance overhaul by a slow and steady approach.

CHAPTER 5

Achieving Organizational Affirmation: The Vote

Now that a date for the congregational decision is on the horizon, it is important to recommend some preparation steps for a decision. If the pastors and leaders are not confident the proposal will pass, it may be time to ensure that all necessary preparations have been made. Just as young men are advised not to ask a girl to marry them if they don't know she'll say yes, the same principle can be applied here. Don't bring something as important as a church structural overhaul to the congregation if you do not have high confidence it will be adopted.

Be sure the leadership base of existing boards and committees agrees to the new structure

My grandfather was a carpenter. When I worked with him on a project he would say, "Measure twice, cut once." That's a good reminder to a pastoral leader attempting to implement the one board governance system. The measure twice admonition is a reminder to double back and be sure the leadership base of your existing boards agrees to the new structure. Until that's done, you can't move forward. In other words, referring back to the concentric circles presented in chapter three, you need to be sure the current ministry leaders are ready for this system to be implemented.

A wise mentor told me that all change is perceived as a loss by some. And so it is with the abandonment of the familiar system of multiple boards and committees in a congregation. Some will view the change as a loss for the church, or possibly the loss of positional leadership for himself or herself. There are some who may misinterpret the motive for change as some sort of power grab by the lead pastor. One must be ready to reassure that, to the contrary, the governing board system can also be called the pastor accountability system. It's a system based on clearly defined strategic objectives for the ministry and a regular accountability to the board on the progress made. Patiently listening to concerns and appropriately responding cannot be overemphasized. The investment of a leader's time and patience will reap huge benefits in the future.

Have supporters verbalize their agreement

As the date for congregational approval of the new bylaws is on the horizon, be sure to have supporters verbalize their agreement. In leadership, there's a time to speak and a time to be silent. But so often congregational leaders have failed to speak up and help the pastor. The time to speak is at both the information meetings and the congregational business meeting.

I can personally remember, on more than one occasion, feeling very vulnerable as questions were being asked from the floor of a business meeting. In those moments, I often desired to hear from one of the congregational leaders who would speak in support of the issue at hand. It's unnerving to think back to the committee room when the support of everyone seemed so apparent, and then to be standing alone in a public meeting wondering where those voices are now. Over the years I've learned the wisdom of asking leaders in advance of a business meeting if they would be willing to speak in favor of a proposal when the need for support becomes obvious. Presenting a new governance structure to the congregation is certainly one of those times.

Some may think I am being overly cautious in recommending that pastors double back to ensure their current leaders are on board with the governance approach. Sadly, I have experienced times when a leader did not express hesitation or disapproval in the setting of a committee meeting, only to stand on the floor of the business meeting and speak against the motion. This is confusing to the voting body and very unnerving and disappointing for the pastor. An important part of leadership is being courageous enough to let your concerns be known in the board room as well as in the public forum, but in the board room first.

Consider adopting a transitional plan if the congregation seems hesitant

In *Winning on Purpose*, John Kaiser advocates an intermediate step in adopting the single governing board system, or what he refers to as Accountable Leadership. He recommends that a temporary suspension of existing bylaws serve as a path by which the new plan can be tested and then adopted.

> This plan places the old bylaws in abeyance, or temporary suspension, for a period of two to three years prior to introducing a new set of bylaws. During the abeyance period, the congregation oper-

ates on the basis of the transition plan in order to allow for a trial run of Accountable Leadership. If Accountable Leadership proves successful, it is confirmed by the adoption of new bylaws. If the transition plan does not produce growth within three years, the congregation can either allow more time or else have the old system back in place. The essence of the Accountable Leadership strategy is incorporated into the transition plan on a temporary basis just as it will be incorporated into the bylaws on a permanent basis after a successful trial run is experienced.[14]

Have a coach present for guidance and perspective at the time of decision making

Depending upon the mood and reputation of the congregation, it may be wise to have a coach present for guidance and perspective at the time of decision making. I would recommend that anytime a congregation is moving into some new or unfamiliar territory, it's good to have an external voice.

It's also helpful to reassure people when you're presenting a new idea that you're not cooking up something nobody's ever heard of before. It's so beneficial to have a coach walk alongside your leaders, to give commentary and reassurance of a very positive experience when implementing the governance system in other churches. Congregations are comforted to learn that many other congregations are implementing a single board governance system with great results.

Conduct a congregational meeting in which the new decision-making structure is approved, and leadership positions are ratified

When a congregational meeting is conducted in which either a transition plan or a new decision-making structure is approved, and leadership positions are ratified, many people mistakenly believe the job is done. But the most crucial part of introducing the governance system is in the last stage I've identified, which is in the implementation.

Experience tells us that without the existence of an implementation plan many motions approved in a business meeting simply die for lack of attention. For example, in the national general assembly meeting of the church body I serve, a study committee presented its recommendation in 2012. The recommendation had to do with the percentage of its income that each local congregation should give to the world-wide work of the church

14 Kaiser, Bandy, Easum, *Winning*, Kindle 2643-2651.

(Support is voluntary in our structure). It was a well-written study, and a motion was made and passed for congregations to comply. Unfortunately, due to the lack of an implementation plan, there was no widespread adoption of the support the study had recommended. The resolution that was passed simply died and now is largely forgotten.

This illustrates the need for a step-by-step implementation plan, which will be discussed in the following chapter.

CHAPTER 6

Implementing a Healthy System

Once the congregation has made a decision to adopt the one-board governance system, the work of implementation is the crucial next step. People will be eager to understand their role in the new system. They will want to understand how it works, and they will need help seeing how a ministry team functions differently than a committee.

In speaking of the confusion caused by the old multiple board and committee structure, one pundit quipped:

The systems we have are perfectly designed for the results we are getting.

Now that the congregation has adopted a new model for organizing its work and attaining decisions, the resulting health in congregational life will begin to show signs of improvement. One person in our Michigan congregation smilingly said, "It feels like we've released the brakes and we're beginning to move!"

Since much of this book is based on my personal experience in implementing the one-board governance system, I am happy to report that once we began working with one board and several ministry teams, we experienced tremendous results. Our congregation seemed to have better focus, more joy in ministry, less red tape, better communication, and a happy governing board. I truly experienced the positive side of this adage. It seemed like a perfect design to support the improved results we were getting.

In response to the before-and-after experience of adopting this new structure, I created an adage of my own:

If you don't organize as the church you intend to be,
you will always be the church you are organized as.

I developed that saying after observing a number of churches start to grow, and then suddenly fall back in size. They would begin growing again, and then once again lose traction. *So, what's holding them back?* I thought. I then began to observe some things about how the church was organized, including the way weekend worship services were organized.

In smaller churches, the Sunday worship service is conducted like an event for a small group of insiders. As prayer time approaches in worship, the leader asks for any prayer requests to be shared. This free-wheeling sharing about prayer concerns and health issues can tend to take several minutes. This is just one example of how a smaller church functions. You have probably noticed that larger churches organize their prayer concerns differently. These needs are usually printed in advance for people to see, and to take home for continued remembrance in prayer. As churches grow, differences are seen in how worship services function, how the board operates, how decisions are made, and how ministry teams function. This is why it is said, "If you don't organize as the church you want to be, you'll always be the church you're organized as."

The focus of this book is on a governance system and bylaws in an effort to foster attitudes toward healthy decision making that doesn't get bogged down in endless committee review, but also provides appropriate accountability for pastoral leaders. This is hugely important for the well-being of a congregation, but there's never just one element that contributes to a church body's health and growth. Most people understand that the quality of worship services, the music, the welcoming atmosphere, the programming for spiritual growth of all ages, outreach to the community, the quality of personal relationships, meaningful small groups, the generosity of God's people, and so much more, contribute to creating the atmosphere for health and growth in the church. Even so, this book is aimed at helping a local pastor train the church board in a healthy way of functioning.

The single board governance system changes the environment of ministry. It allows for a large group of lay people to be focused on ministry teams and outreach to the community more than attending committee meetings and spending evenings in a church classroom, reading minutes, voting on matters, and sending recommendations to other committees.

Those who garden know that a big part of gardening is providing an environment with lots of sunshine, appropriate amounts of water, an absence of weeds to choke out the growth, and the right kind of fertilizer. When the soil is right, the temperature is right, the water is available, and all the elements come together, a magnificent fruit and vegetable-bearing garden is the result. In similar fashion, the single board governance systems provide a health-producing environment in the church.

Implementation Step 1:
Conduct a leadership event to launch the new system

One of the biggest mistakes made is the failure to conduct a leadership event for implementation. Although people may have affirmatively voted to accept new bylaws and a new philosophy of decision making, it should not be assumed that church members fully understand how this will affect church life and culture. A gathering of church leaders for refreshments or a shared meal will provide an open atmosphere for describing how the governance system will work. In my experience, one of the most confusing concepts for volunteers to grasp is the difference between a ministry team and a committee. Sample agendas comparing a ministry huddle to a committee meeting can be helpful. Most people want to understand what their role is in the new system. The subject of power is likely to surface. People want reassurance that their voice will continue to matter as future ministries and changes are considered.

It is at this point that a helpful illustration developed by Rod Stafford in his book, *Free to Lead,* can be introduced.[15]

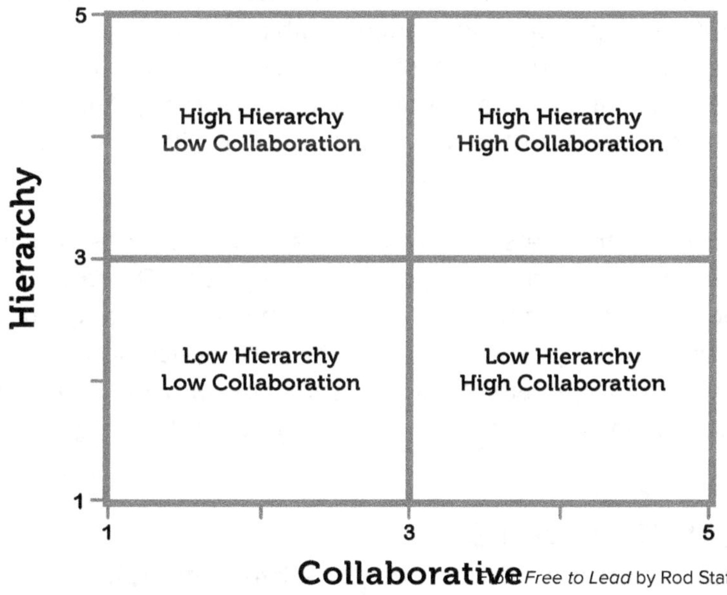

From *Free to Lead* by Rod Stafford.

In this illustration, the top left corner represents an autocratic or dictatorial atmosphere. The bottom left corner depicts an apathetic group. In that

15 Stafford, *Free to Lead*, 25.

group, no one is in charge and everyone participates according to their own estimation of right decisions. This situation brings to mind this verse of Scripture: *In those days Israel had no king; all the people did whatever seemed right in their own eyes* (Judges 17:6).

The bottom right corner represents an atmosphere devoid of leadership in which much discussion takes place, everyone's opinions count equally, but very few decisions are made and forward progress is stalled. The top right corner is the aspirational goal of the collaborative hierarchy. It is an atmosphere where a clear decision maker is identified, yet it is obvious to everyone that the decision maker seeks input and perspective from others in making decisions. The decision maker remains accountable to the governing board, yet is free to lead in the manner that brings the most health and forward progress to the organization.

Implementation Step 2:
Consider having a coach present to help launch and guide the governing board in its new role

The growing prevalence of the governance board and staff accountability system means there is an ever-increasing number of pastors and church leaders who have experience in working within it. I strongly encourage those seeking to implement this system to invite a leader to serve as a coach during your implementation time. There are many questions that can best be answered by others who are familiar with how the system functions.

It is most helpful if the persons invited to serve as nonresident board members have worked within the governance system. Those individuals would be good choices as coaches as they will have an ongoing presence as part of your governing board. Without this vital coaching and orientation, there is a great risk that the board will slip backward into management concerns rather than a higher vision-based approach to the goals of the ministry.

Implementation Step 3:
Share a vision from the pulpit: everyone has a ministry

One of the greatest opportunities to expand the ministry of the congregation has now been settled. It is up to the lead pastor to help each member of the church understand that no longer does one have to be elected to serve on a committee in order to participate in the work and ministry of the church. Teaching on 1 Corinthians, chapter 1, regarding God's distribution of gifts to the church body is applicable here, as is teaching from 1 Peter 2:5 (NIV): *You also, like living stones, are being built into a spiritual house to be a holy priesthood, offering spiritual sacrifices acceptable to God through Jesus Christ.* While the purpose of this book is to reorganize and unleash individuals for the cooperative work of Christ within the church body, it cannot be forgotten that the ultimate purpose of the church exists outside its doors. We must continually ask, "How can we extend our ministry within our community?"

Noted statesman of the church, R. Eugene Sterner reminds us:

> The church as an institution cannot enter the marketplace or business or politics except as it does so through chosen individuals who are prepared and trained for their task. But if the whole church is a ministry now gathered together for worship, now dispersed into the marketplace, the shop, and the office, then obviously the church is going by its representatives into countless areas where the Christian witness takes place.[16]

Implementation Step 4:
Give public thanks to those who have served on committees

It is wise to remember that all change is perceived as a loss by some. Therefore, the abandonment of the familiar committee structure in the church is bound to feel like a loss or a demotion to some individuals. Pastors and church leaders will do well to highlight the work of various committees, to give public recognition to those who have served, and to encourage others to join them in the new ministry team approach.

It is important to remind others that the change in bylaws doesn't mean that structure is not needed. Nor does the change mean that voting and decisions are not needed. The new system has been implemented to provide for healthy structure and healthy decisions. Remind the congregation that a new climate encourages new growth. It's a time for new ministries, new creativity, and new determination to fulfill God's purpose for the local congregation.

This new way of thinking contributes to a fresh new climate of church life, in which ministry is no longer bogged down in endless committee meetings. Perhaps you have had the experience of discussing the same subject for consecutive months, without any action being accomplished. Repeating the same topic again can lead to feelings of futility. Why are we meeting?

16 R. Eugene Sterner, *You Have a Ministry*, Warner Press, Anderson, IN, 1963, 101.

Why can't we move forward? When people have experienced these common frustrations repeatedly, they view a fresh approach to ministry with enthusiasm.

The ministry teams created by a new structure provide freedom to make decisions, and to accomplish ministry in ways that begin to have a ripple effect in the whole congregation. One example of a new ministry launched outside the bureaucracy of the committee structure is One Heart in Dayton, Ohio.

A woman named Donna at Salem Church developed a burden in her heart for the young women dancers in the adult entertainment industry who become trapped in the sex industry. Since many of these young women believe the church hates them, Donna resolved to express love and compassion to them in the name of Jesus.

On her own, she began a ministry called One Heart, knowing that such an endeavor was unlikely to ever be approved through the typical church committee structure. She takes gifts and casseroles into the clubs in an effort to minister to young women. They call her Mama Donna. Her mission statement is to love these young women until they finally ask her why. Over a period of several years, women from the church have joined her effort to minister and redeem lives. The network of women who prepare meals and provide gifts has greatly expanded. The fruit of the ministry includes young women who have left the sex industry, become college graduates, and reestablished their lives. Some of the young women now live in apartments furnished through the efforts of the men of the church.

This is the kind of outward-focused ministry that can happen when the church functions with ministry teams instead of committees. Eventually the One Heart ministry was included in the church mission budget and has become an important outreach of the congregation. The staff of the Salem church fulfill a supportive role, but do not strive to dictate or direct the ministry.

Such is the life-changing effect of ministry that is embraced by members of a local congregation outside of the requirements of endless debate and approval processes. This new freedom for innovative and creative ministry bears fruit and shows positive outcomes. As a result, church leaders soon begin to realize that they have adopted a better way!

Implementation Step 5:
Construct the first governing board wisely

Our first governing board was an amalgamation of leaders from council/trustees/etc. When moving from a long-standing traditional structure consisting of a church council, a board of trustees, and possibly a board of finance, it is wise to compose the first governing board as an amalgamation of individuals with gifts and perspectives. This is reassuring, not only to those asked to serve, but to the church body also. The bylaws will call for a rotation of terms, so it is recommended that the first governing board initially be composed of some with one-year terms, others with two-year terms, and still others with three-year terms. When the terms expire, each will be replaced by three-year terms, and the rotation cycle is then established. The illustration below shows how the term rotation works.

	YEAR 1	YEAR 2	YEAR 3	YEAR 4	YEAR 5	YEAR 6
POSITION 1	1	Renewed 3-Year Term			New 3-Year Term	
POSITION 2	1	2	New 3-Year Term			Renewed
POSITION 3	1	2	3	New 3-Year Term		
POSITION 4	1	New 3-Year Term			Renewed 3-Year Term	
POSITION 5	1	New 3-Year Term			Renewed 3-Year Term	
POSITION 6	1	2	Renewed 3-Year Term			New
POSITION 7	1	2	3	Renewed 3-Year Term		

Implementation Step 6:
Construct the governing board agenda wisely

One of the biggest changes to be experienced is the new pattern of board meetings and the release of day-to-day management to the staff team. A great principle to remember here is the eight-word overview of governance: Pastor leads. Staff manages. Board governs. People minister. Certainly, there were times when I asked the governing board to advise—to give their helpful perspective regarding leadership dilemmas or matters requiring a broad perspective. I kept the governing board informed about the health of the entire ministry by giving very thorough quarterly reports from the senior pastor. The board gave me freedom to lead, and good accountability to keep priorities on track. Kaiser's *Winning on Purpose* provides helpful perspective about the agenda and the frequency of meetings:

> The board invests its precious time and energy to govern the big picture. To leverage that investment, I recommend that church boards hold their regular meetings on a quarterly basis. Boards can still call a special meeting if an action is both necessary and urgent. And they can act upon less important urgencies by telephone, email, or video conference. By contrast, the staff should meet far more frequently—weekly and/or monthly—in order to function as the center of ministry coordination. There are several reasons for quarterly board meetings under normal circumstances: 1) Meeting more often than necessary tempts a board to manage rather than govern. 2) Meeting less often than necessary tempts a board to abdicate rather than govern. 3) Most boards will govern most effectively by holding two to six carefully prepared meetings each year. 4) The staff should meet much more often than the board to coordinate the details of management.[17]

The ministry staff now serves in a system that removes hurdles and empowers them to make decisions within the parameters established by the governing board. The board does not endanger the whole ministry by relinquishing all control. It empowers staff to make ministry decisions and expend church funds within the confines allowed by cash flow and limitations established by board policies. This is an important contrast to the former requirement of seeking permission from the board to make expenditures of already budgeted funds. This pro-leadership atmosphere helps the board agenda expand its focus beyond a preoccupation with finances.

Implementation Step 7:
Make quarterly board meetings a quality event

In launching a new governing board system in our Michigan congregation, I decided to make the quarterly board meetings memorable events. We decided to begin the evening at 5:00 PM with a catered meal. A local restaurant provided excellent cuisine at an affordable rate. A delicious dessert was always included. My administrative assistant accepted the responsibility to create a nice environment for the meetings. She used nice tablecloths and seasonally appropriate centerpieces and decorations. Soft background music and adjusted lighting contributed to a "wow" experience for the board members. We used two classrooms, adjacent to one another, so the meal could be served in the first room, and we would then migrate to the second room for the meeting. We did our best to honor our

17 Kaiser, Bandy, Easum, *Winning*, Kindle 2532-2541.

board members by creating a wonderful dinner experience to show our appreciation. This set a tone of professionalism and built a sense of anticipation for our quarterly meetings.

We learned that by beginning the evening with a professional atmosphere, the attitude carried over into the business session. The fellowship time over an excellent meal seemed to erase whatever stress our board members carried in from their workplace and set a positive tone for the entire evening. Usually our business sessions went from 6:30–8:30 PM. Occasionally, the meetings were extended until 9:00 PM.

Once this new format for meetings was introduced, my personal anticipation of the quarterly meeting was heightened. I could hardly wait for our nonresident board members to arrive at the airport, or to drive in from out of town. The entire event felt festive and celebrative. I confess that I dreaded the old management style of board meetings. This new way of operating felt like the best of times. I was enthusiastic about sharing the lead pastor's quarterly report concerning the health of the ministry. I was eager to receive perspective and insights from board members. I was thankful for the times of prayer. All of these elements converged to produce an encouraging, life-giving meeting. I went home feeling uplifted, supported, affirmed, and like the church was moving forward. I know most pastors and leaders do not go home from church board meetings with such a positive feeling.

Once the governing board system is implemented, those involved in the new healthy decision-making culture usually state that it feels like a culture of trust and appropriate accountability. I continue to celebrate every congregation that launches this structure. I see it as a better way, a productive way, and a meaningful way to accomplish Christ's ministry through a local church.

CHAPTER 7

Avoiding Misfires and Failures

While consulting with a group of pastors and church leaders about the one-board governance model, I was asked to candidly divulge whether or not there have been disappointments and points of distresses in churches where a governance system was introduced. I appreciated the encouragement to share transparently and will also use this chapter to describe some of the difficulties I've observed as church leaders transition to a new way of working together. Keep in mind, I am not always present to personally observe all the dynamics in play when various churches have implemented this system. Yet, I have been able to identify some "landmines" or reasons that churches have experienced some difficulties.

Misfire 1:
Lack of board orientation and training

Even the casual observer can easily recognize most pastors and lay leaders in the church have never received training in effective board functions. 2 Timothy 3:5 describes people in the last days as *having a form of godliness but denying its power.* In like manner, I have seen congregations who have a form of governance but deny its power. Due to lack of training, most boards limp along doing the things people assume a board should be doing, but most often are making crucial errors that largely hamper the work of the church.

A large selection of books, videos, and training resources exist to guide church leaders into a practical understanding of governance. In my own experience, I found it was necessary to patiently explain on multiple occasions the responsibilities and limitations of the board. It takes some time for a group of lay leaders to get the hang of governing. My attempts to have board members read training materials were usually unsuccessful; consequently, I began to conduct an annual board orientation and training session during the first board meeting after the annual business meeting, when newly ratified members joined the board. This provided training for new board members and important ongoing reminders for existing members.

Misfire 2:
Slipping back into managing instead of governing

It's important that the governing board keep their eyes on empowering the mission of the congregation. The temptation is strong to slide back into functioning like a management board. Take, for example, the desire to discuss the programming or worship service schedule of the church. These issues, along with maintenance schedules, repairs, and the regular purchases of supplies are no longer the purview of the governing board. These are management-level decisions that are made at other levels of the organization. Inevitably a board will tend to begin discussing matters of management. We referred to such detours as getting off the main path and into the weeds. Eventually, it became common for board members to self-police the board's business when someone would declare, "Hey, we're getting off into the weeds again!"

Misfire 3:
Failure to value the benefit of nonresident board members

Chapter 3 clearly states the benefits of having nonresident board members at the table. The wisdom and perspective to be gleaned from them is invaluable. I have observed that some churches elect to forego this opportunity. Sometimes it is a financial decision to avoid the added expense of reimbursement for travel and lodging. Other times, there is resistance from church members to "outsiders" speaking into local church concerns. The pastor and lay leaders may decide it is not worth the trouble to try to convince the inconvincible. Each of these reasons is shortsighted, however, and every attempt should be made to find a way to incorporate the valuable input of nonresident board members.

Misfire 4:
Pastor neglectful of communicating decisions

While great freedom is given to the pastor to lead, with that freedom comes great responsibility. The governance-accountability system is built on trust. It assumes that the leader of the organization is trustworthy and adept in matters of leadership. No longer is it necessary to navigate multiple layers of approval for every decision. I've observed, however, that the great responsibility the pastor must accept is to communicate appropriately and to keep the board informed. In some congregations, there has been stress when the pastor (and staff) have failed to understand the importance of communicating and keeping the board in the loop about decisions being made. This could be remedied by creating a systematic reporting system between board meetings for keeping the board up to speed with operational decisions being made. In my experience, as the church begins to grow, the pace of life and decision making begins to increase exponentially. This is when the board begins to feel "out of the loop." Therefore, a communication system should be created and implemented to avoid that perception. When a communication system is not in place, the issue is often described as "too much power" in the pastoral office. The real issue, in fact, is not "too much power" but "lack of communication."

Keeping the constituency of the church informed is one more important responsibility. I have heard, for instance, of remodeling to the church building being launched and catching many congregants off-guard. Certainly, the freedom to make the decision existed, yet a good public relations approach demands keeping the rank and file members of the organization in the communication loop. After all, these constituents are the donors that make the remodeling possible.

The methods of communication and keeping people informed may vary. I found it to be extremely helpful to everyone when I wrote a regular pastor's column in our church newsletter (which later became a digital e-newsletter). A few paragraphs helped people see the rationale for decisions being made, and the more I communicated, the greater the trust grew. I've included an excerpt from a weekly pastoral column in the summer of 2012 as an example of my communication to the congregation.

> "Next" is a word that builds anticipation. "What's next?" is a question we all frequently hear.
>
> Salem Church is ready for the next phase of our life as a congregation. Momentum has been building throughout the summer months, and we are all looking forward to moving back into our main auditorium on Sunday, September 9th.
>
> I'm anticipating that you will be thrilled by the new look and the new sound in our sanctuary. The clarity of the new sound system is amazing. The lighting and video equipment have experienced major upgrades. You'll be pleased.
>
> We're looking forward to the next stage of growth in our outreach. The next stage of growth in our small group ministry. We're literally preparing for and expecting the next wave of growth at Salem!
>
> How can you help? I'm glad you asked. Help us prepare for the next

great day of celebration as we move into our renovated auditorium on September 9th. We need our entire church family to be present to help us celebrate! It's going to be a fantastic day!

Are you ready for what's next?

Enthusiastically,
Pastor Moss

Leaders should use whatever means of communication best fits their own situation. Some rely on social media, others create video announcements. The principle to remember is the high level of importance placed on good communication to the constituent base. Simply put, good communication enhances trust. The lack of communication erodes trust.

Misfire 5:
Board members feeling disconnected

It should not be a surprise to learn that some governing board members, accustomed to a monthly meeting regimen, expressed a feeling of disconnect from "knowing what's going on" when a quarterly meeting schedule was introduced. At least two board members asked that we return to a more frequent meeting schedule. I knew that it would be problematic for two reasons. First, the nonresident board members could not incorporate more frequent meetings into their schedule. Secondly, more meetings would automatically cause the board to return to a management mindset rather than a governance approach. At my suggestion, a compromise was made. We continued with the four quarterly meetings of the governing board. Additionally, we met six times per year in the prayer room near the sanctuary, to pray specifically to support the ministry of the church. I spent time updating the board members on prayer needs among various staff and ministry departments. This became a meaningful gathering for pastors and board members. We did not meet at all during July. In December, our gathering was a fellowship and dessert night at my home. In all, the governing board was together ten times each year with four business sessions and six prayer gatherings.

Misfire 6:
The erosion of collaboration

Chapter 3 discusses the importance of creating an atmosphere of collaboration. It describes how, in a collaborative hierarchy, the lead pastor has the authority to overrule the preferences or recommendations of the staff team but sees the wisdom in listening to the voices of others. The point is, the staff team has some observations that will help the lead pastor make better decisions. The sense of value and esteem increases in an organization when the voices of others are included in the decision-making mix. Conversely, when the leader becomes busy, distracted, or too preoccupied to seek the input of others, the sense of frustration grows. All-too-soon the leader is viewed, not as collaborative, but as an independent decision maker.

Throughout the book the subject of healthy decision making has been promoted. Every leader needs to be reminded that health must be intentionally maintained, whether it be physical health, emotional health, spiritual health, or organizational health. Maintaining collaboration is an important part of keeping the organization healthy.

Misfire 7:
Failure to establish evaluation benchmarks for performance reviews

One of the most important building blocks of the one-board governance system is the commitment of the governing board to hold their one employee accountable for leading the organization towards the fulfillment of its goals. This presupposes that the lead pastor and the governing board have worked together to establish goals, clarify their meaning, and create a clearly defined path toward their achievement. Each quarterly board meeting should be an opportunity for the pastor to give updates to the board on the progress toward the goals, as well as to communicate any roadblocks and hurdles along the way. In turn, the board should be seeking ways to facilitate the leader's success.

The board should ensure that the lead pastor's job description plus the organizational goals are clearly stated and can be used for periodic evaluation and performance review. In my experience, unless the periodic review is scheduled on the board's annual calendar, it is unlikely to occur. Without this vital accountability and feedback, goals get sidelined and the leader gets distracted from his or her job description to spending energy on secondary concerns. Another important value to explore in a periodic review is whether or not the pastor is functioning in a collaborative manner. This question can be explored with the leader—and possibly with his or her subordinates.

Misfire 8:
Failure to seek legal review

As conscientious people, we want to steward ministry funds with wisdom and discretion. But, it is not prudent to economize and sidestep having an attorney review the new bylaws before they are passed by the congregation. In reading the sample bylaws, it may seem that everything is in order; however, the laws vary from state to state. *Lost in Logistics* is not intended to give legal advice. It is intended to introduce principles and to provide anecdotal evidence of how those principles have benefited congregations. When preparing new bylaws and a new decision-making structure, it's important to be sure that:

- the bylaws are in compliance with state laws
- the bylaws are in harmony with the congregation's Articles of Incorporation or other documents on file with the state government

A FINAL WORD

Having spent nearly all of my adult life in pastoral ministry, I want to end *Lost in Logistics* with some words of pastoral encouragement. There is no doubt in my mind that you are overwhelmed with all that is required to move your church board from its present condition into a vibrant and healthy governing board. This is why I've tried to present a step-by-step approach in this book. I am certain the very first step is a step of faith. You must have faith to believe that Jesus Christ desires for every expression of his body—the church—to function optimally, without unnecessary hindrances or hurdles. Trust the Lord to show you the perfect time and the perfect way to introduce these concepts to your board. Allow yourself to believe that the leaders of your congregation also hope for a better way. You don't have to take the journey alone. Many congregations across the land are beginning to experience the health that comes from this governance-accountability structure. Ask capable leaders to come alongside and introduce these concepts to your church. Begin the journey toward the new day God has in store for your ministry. Once you do, you'll never look back!

APPENDIX 1

Byrum Sample Bylaws

BYLAWS OF THE ______________________________CHURCH OF GOD

LOCATED AT ____

Article I

NAME

This organization shall be called the (Name)______________________________[18]

Church of God of (Address)______________________________________

Article II

PURPOSE

The object of the association as organized under these bylaws is to control and facilitate the business activities of this church in such matters as the acquiring and holding of real estate, in the collecting and disbursing of money, and in the appointing and directing of agencies for these and other purposes. The purpose of this association is to deal with the business affairs only of the church. It shall pass no resolution having to do with the doctrines or the religious customs and practices of the church or its members.

Article III

MEMBERSHIP

Section 1. Only those may become members of this organization who are recognized as members of the local congregation and who are more than twenty-one years of age.

Section 2. The secretary shall keep a list of the names of members of this business organization of the church, which list shall be revised before each annual meeting, by the pastor and its officers, by adding names of new members of the church and striking out names of those who have for any cause ceased to be members of the local congregation.

Section 3. This revised list shall be subject to ratification by this body at the beginning of its annual meeting.

Section 4. The rules governing membership herein stated, shall apply to the business organization only, and shall not affect in any way the standing of members in the ecclesiastical body. (Those who prefer another method of defining membership may substitute for the foregoing article three, the following. The foregoing, however, has the advantage of greater definiteness of membership and may be used, probably with modifications, if the organization is to be incorporated.)

18 Churches in small places may be named after the town, in larger places, after the street or section. If a church is the first Church of God in the city, it may be so designated. Other designations may be used.

Alternate Article III

MEMBERSHIP

Section 1. All the members of the (Name) ______________________ Church of God at (Address) ______________________________________ shall have the right to vote in its business meetings, except as herein provided:

- **a)** They must be sixteen years of age or over.
- **b)** They must have worshipped regularly with this Church for a period of at least six months.
- **c)** They must have lived during that period of six months in harmony with the doctrines and practices of the Church of God. Any member may be given the right to vote by a two-thirds majority of the members present, regardless of the foregoing conditions.

Section 2. If any member's right to vote in a business meeting of this church is questioned and said member insists that he has the right to vote, then the objector may call for an expression of the assembly and the chairman shall ask members present in said business meeting to cast a vote, and the majority of the members voting shall determine the questioned member's right and be binding upon all.

Section 3. If a member's right to vote is not questioned, such silence on the part of all shall be taken as prima facie evidence of said member's right to vote.

Section 4. An objection to any member's right to vote may be raised at any time before the actual voting is called for by the chair, and any member may call upon the presiding official before a vote is cast to require each person present to signify whether he considers himself qualified to vote.

Section 5. The rules and regulations governing membership herin stated shall apply to business meetings only, and shall not affect in any way the religious rights and privileges of the members.

Article IV

OFFICERS

Section 1. The officers of the business meeting of the church shall be a chairman, a vice-chairman, a secretary, and a treasurer.

Section 2. The regularly chosen pastor of the congregation by virtue of his office shall also be chairman of the business meetings of the church. As chairman, he shall preside at all business meetings of the church and exercise a general supervision over the business affairs of the church.

Section 3. The vice-chairman shall perform the duties of the chairman in his absence, or in the event of his inability to serve as chairman.

Section 4. The secretary shall keep an orderly record of the proceedings of the business meetings of the church in a book provided for that purpose. This book shall be carefully preserved by him and shall remain the property of the church.

Section 5. The treasurer shall receive the funds of the church and administer them as hereinafter set forth in cooperation with two other persons who with him shall compose a finance committee.

Section 6. The elected officers—vice chairman, secretary, and treasurer, shall be elected for a term of one year. They shall serve from the close of the meeting at which they are elected to the close of the meeting at which their successors are elected. These officers must be elected from among the members of this organization. They shall be elected at the same time and in the same manner as are members of committees.

Article V
COMMITTEES

Section 1. STANDING COMMITTEES. The standing committees of the church are four in number: a board of trustees, a finance committee, a benevolence committee, and a budget committee.

Section 2. BOARD OF TRUSTEES. The trustees of the Church shall be five in number.[19] Their duties shall be to hold in trust all the property of the church in accordance with the laws of the State. They shall function subject to and under the direction of church. Their duties as trustees shall not include the choosing and placing of spiritual workers in the church. All questions pertaining to doctrine, ecclesiastical forms and usages, and the conduct of its religious services shall be determined by the recognized spiritual leadership of the church. They shall appoint as officers from among themselves a chairman or president, a secretary, and a treasurer.

Section 3. FINANCE COMMITTEE.[20] The finance committee shall consist of three[21] members, two elected, and the church treasurer shall be an ex officio member and treasurer of this committee. It shall have charge under the direction of the church of the collecting and disbursing of the money of the church. It shall earnestly endeavor to collect the amount of money required to meet the estimated needs of the church for its fiscal year and as much more as possible for benevolent purposes. This money shall be disbursed according to the annual church budget or other instructions of the church when given. It shall appoint from among its members a chairman. The treasurer, who is also the treasurer of the church, shall deposit the funds of the church in whatever bank, or banks, may be recommended by the committee. He shall be authorized to receipt all monies paid to the church. The deposit account of the church, wherever kept, shall be in the name of the church. He shall cause all vouchers and orders paid by him to be filed and to be properly preserved as a part of the records of the church. He shall furnish the chairman a detailed statement of the receipts and disbursements of the church's monies received and disbursed by him during any period, when requested to do so. His books shall at all times be open to inspection by the other members of the committee and by the members of the church. He shall sign all checks drawn on the account of the church, and shall turn over money to the treasurer of the board of trustees or other agents of the church according to the church's direction.

19 A larger number is desirable in large churches.

20 The trustees may serve as the finance committee also, but a separate committee is usually better. If but one committee is desired for both phases of work, then the same persons may be elected on both committees.

21 In very large churches five or more.

Section 4. BENEVOLENCE COMMITTEE. The Benevolence Committee shall consist of three members. Its duties shall be to acquaint itself with the circumstances of those of the community who are properly objects of charity, and to wisely distribute among such the funds of the church which are set aside for this purpose.

Section 5. BUDGET COMMITTEE. This committee shall consist of the combined membership of the Board of Trustees, Finance Committee and the Benevolence Committee; also, the chairman, vice-chairman, and the secretary of the church business organization. The chairman of the church business organization shall act as chairman, and the treasurer of the church as secretary. The duties of the Budget Committee shall be to arrange a budget of the estimated expenses of the congregation for its next fiscal year and then submit it to the church for ratification.

Section 6. SPECIAL COMMITTEES. Special committees shall be appointed to perform any special service needed. These may be of such size and appointed in such manner as the church may choose at the time.

Section 7. NOMINATIONS. Nominations for committees and officers of the business meeting shall be made by a committee of five appointed by the pastor, the elected officers of the business meeting, and the presiding officer of each of the standing elected committees.[22] This committee shall nominate not fewer than two persons for each vacancy to be filled. Nominations shall be only of those who are qualified to vote in the business meetings of the church.

Section 8. ELECTIONS. All officers and standing committees of the church shall be elected by ballot at the annual meeting of the church. Members of standing committees shall be elected for terms of three years, but their terms at first shall be for one, two and three years, that the terms of one third of the members of each elected committee shall expire each year. The term of newly elected members of committees and of officers of committees shall begin with the fiscal year of the church.

Article VI
MEETINGS

Section 1. REGULAR. The annual business meeting of the church shall be held at the church building on the first Wednesday (or other day of the week) in the month of ____________________, and notice of such meeting shall be given in a regular meeting of the church by the chairman or vice-chairman of the church business meeting at least one week prior to that time.

Section 2. SPECIAL. A special business meeting of the church may be called at any time by the chairman. Upon the written request of five members, stating the purpose for which they desire the meeting called, the chairman shall call a special meeting of the church. For any special meeting of the church to be held, the chairman shall give at least seven days' notice, figured from the time the notice is given. Said notice shall state the object of calling such special meeting and give the date and place for holding the same. The special business meetings may be held in connection with any meetings for worship or other purposes.

22 In small churches this committee may be appointed by the pastor subject to ratification by the church.

Article VII
ORDER OF BUSINESS

Section 1. The order of business at all meetings of the church shall be as follows:

1. Prayer
2. Roll call
3. Reading of the minutes of the last meeting
4. Reports of officers
5. Reports of committees
6. Unfinished business
7. Dismissals, or elections of successors
8. Original resolutions and new business

Article VIII
BYLAWS

Section 1. The secretary shall cause that these bylaws be printed or typewritten, and a copy thereof be given or sent to each officer and committee. After every meeting of the church in which any revision or amendments of the bylaws are made, the secretary shall cause a new edition to be published and a copy of the revised bylaws to be delivered or mailed to each trustee.

Article IX
EXPULSION

Section 1. Any officer of this body or any member of any regular or special board or committee which it may constitute may be expelled from his office by a three-fourths vote of the members present at any regular or special meeting. Such expulsion may be for conduct unbecoming to a member of the Church of God, for failure of duty, a lack of interest and zeal in the work of the church, for adhering to a doctrine contrary to that held by the church, or for other reasons the congregation deem sufficient grounds for expulsion from his office.

Section 2. Notice of the time of the meeting for expulsion and the reason for expulsion shall be given at least seven days prior to the date of the meeting. A written statement of the charges against the person to be expelled shall be given to him by the secretary of the church not later than the time of the meeting before his expulsion is announced. When one has been expelled from his office, his authority in the business of the church ceases at once.

Article X

QUORUM

Section 1. Fifty[23] members shall constitute a quorum at all business meetings of the church.

Article XI

AMENDMENTS

Section 1. These Bylaws may be amended, altered, or changed by a three-fourths vote of the entire membership of the church present at any regular or special meeting of the church, and a copy of the proposed amendment, alteration, or change, and notice that action will be taken thereon, shall be read publicly at least fourteen days prior to such regular or special meeting.

23 The number should depend upon the size of the congregation. It should not be fewer than one half of the total membership of the church business body.

APPENDIX 2

Sample Bylaws

Constitution & Bylaws of the ______________________ CHURCH OF GOD
CITY, STATE

PREAMBLE

The Constitution and Bylaws contained herein are designed to govern the business and legal affairs of this Corporation. They are intended to be in harmony with Biblical principles (see Exodus 18:12-27, Exodus 25-40, Nehemiah 1-13, Matthew 22:37-40, Acts 1:12-26, Acts 4:33-35, Acts 6:1-7, Acts 14:23, Acts 20:17, 28, 1 Corinthians 12, 2 Corinthians 8, Ephesians 4:11-16, 1 Timothy 3:1-13, Titus 1:5-9) and implemented under the guidance of God's Holy Spirit in an attitude of Christian love. In matters not specifically addressed in the Bylaws, the Corporation will continue to be guided by the Holy Spirit in keeping with Biblical principles.

ARTICLE I. NAME

In order to govern the business and legal affairs of this church, the members agree to form a Corporation which shall operate in accordance with this Constitution and Bylaws. The name of this Corporation shall be _____ Church of God Inc., CITY, STATE. The address is ____________ ______________________. This Corporation is affiliated with the Church of God Reformation Movement with general offices in Anderson, Indiana.

ARTICLE II. PURPOSE

The purpose of this Corporation shall be to help persons experience transformation through the love of Jesus Christ and to express that love to others so that they may also be transformed.

ARTICLE III. MEMBERSHIP

Section 3.1 MEMBERS of this Corporation shall be those who are confessing Christians, are in accord with the doctrines and tenants of the _____Church of God, CITY, STATE, and consider this their church home.

Section 3.2 VOTING MEMBERS Those eligible to vote in business meetings of this Corporation shall meet the following conditions:

- **A.** They must consider themselves members of this Corporation as defined in Article III, Section 3.1.
- **B.** They must have attended services of this Corporation regularly for at least three of the four months immediately preceding the business meeting at which they exercise the right to vote. Members with a second home, out-of-state, may be approved to vote by notifying the church office. This list will be given to the Corporation Secretary for record-keeping.
- **C.** They must be at least 16 years of age.

D. The foregoing rules governing voting membership shall apply only to business meetings of the Corporation and shall not affect in any way the ecclesiastical fellowship of the Corporation.

ARTICLE IV. PRINCIPLES OF GOVERNANCE

Section 4.1 CONGREGATIONAL VOTES Recognizing the role of the Corporation in discerning the will of God in major decisions of the church, the following items shall require a congregational vote in a duly called business meeting of the Corporation:

1. Call of a Senior Pastor
2. Purchase or sale of real property or buildings
3. Incurring of long-term debt in excess of three years and/or a per year amount in excess of 5% of the Annual General Operating Budget
4. Approval of the Annual General Operating Budget
5. Individual Ratification of Governing Board Members
6. Alteration, amendment or repeal of the Constitution & Bylaws

Individual ratification shall require a three-fourths (75%) majority of those Voting Members present and absentee ballots, unless otherwise stated within the Bylaws.

Section 4.2 GENERAL MANAGEMENT AND OVERSIGHT Recognizing the role of spiritual authority and leadership in the life of the church, the Corporation entrusts to the Senior Pastor and staff of the Corporation the authority to manage both the corporate and spiritual affairs of the church under the control and oversight of the Governing Board.

ARTICLE V. QUALIFICATIONS FOR LEADERSHIP

The Senior Pastor, pastoral and ministry staff of the Corporation shall be confessing Christians and live lives that reflect holiness and manifest the fruits of the spirit. He or she shall be well respected within their own family, their church, their profession and their community. He or she shall have a warm welcoming spirit, a positive attitude and be able to see the good both in people and in situations. He or she shall tithe to and be regular attendees in worship at __________ Church of God, CITY, STATE.

ARTICLE VI. AMENDMENTS

The Constitution and Bylaws may be altered, amended, replaced or repealed by a three-fourths majority vote of Voting Members present and voting, including approved absentee ballots, at any duly called Annual or Special Business Meeting of the Corporation. Copies of the proposed amendments shall be made available at least two weeks prior to the Informational Meeting(s) along with the Article(s) and Section(s) to be altered, amended, replaced or repealed.

ARTICLE VII. DISTRIBUTION OF PROPERTY UPON DISSOLUTION

In the event of the dissolution of this Corporation or the severing of its affiliation with the Church of God, Anderson, IN, no officer, Governing Board Member(s), employee, Corporation member, or any private individual shall be entitled to share in the disposition of the assets of the Corporation, and all its assets shall become the property of (***choose: Church of God Ministries, Inc., Anderson, IN/or State Ministries***) or its successor. *(Choice is made in consideration of capacity of receiving organization to properly deal with assets.)*

BYLAWS

ARTICLE I. OFFICERS OF THE CORPORATION

Section 1.1 SENIOR PASTOR AND CHIEF EXECUTIVE OFFICER

A. The Senior Pastor shall provide Biblical vision and leadership for the Corporation and shall preside over the daily spiritual and business affairs of the Corporation. By virtue of office, the Senior Pastor shall be President of the Corporation.

B. The Senior Pastor, or his or her designates, shall provide oversight and direction to all staff and ministry leaders; set policies and procedures for the establishment, operation and elimination of ministries; and approve all lay ministers and volunteers operating on behalf of the Corporation.

C. The Senior Pastor hires and dismisses pastoral staff, subject to the approval of the Governing Board. The Senior Pastor, or his or her designates, hires and dismisses all other program or support staff. Any staff person who has been dismissed may appeal the dismissal to the Governing Board. The decision of the Governing Board shall be final.

D. The Senior Pastor shall have authority to call Business Meetings of the Corporation, and shall preside at all Business Meetings of the Corporation. In the absence of the Senior Pastor at any Business Meeting, the Chairperson of the Governing Board shall chair the Business Meeting.

E. The Senior Pastor shall present the Annual General Operating Budget to the Governing Board for approval prior to its presentation to the Corporation for approval.

Section 1.2 CHAIRPERSON OF THE GOVERNING BOARD The Chairperson of the Governing Board shall preside over any Business Meeting of the Corporation in the absence of the Senior Pastor and, by virtue of office, shall serve as the Vice President of the Corporation. During times of transition in the Senior Pastoral Leadership, the Chairperson may call Special Business Meetings of the Corporation.

Section 1.3 TREASURER OF THE CORPORATION The Treasurer of the Governing Board shall, by virtue of his or her office, also serve as Treasurer of the Corporation. The Treasurer shall be responsible for monitoring and safeguarding the financial assets of the Corporation, ensuring sound internal controls and financial policies, signing checks in the absence of staff, or where an officer's signature is required. The Treasurer shall also designate authorized signatories and is responsible for directing the dissemination of regular financial reports by staff to the Corporation.

Section 1.4 SECRETARY OF THE CORPORATION The Secretary of the Governing Board shall, by virtue of his or her office, also serve as Secretary of the Corporation. The Secretary shall ensure that all minutes of the business meetings of the Corporation are properly recorded and made available for future reference.

ARTICLE II. GOVERNING BOARD

Section 2.1 GOVERNING BOARD MEMBERSHIP The Governing Board shall be composed of not less than nine or more than twelve members individually ratified by the Corporation, plus the Senior Pastor, who is an ex-officio, non-voting member. Two members of the Governing Board shall be chosen from outside of the Corporation. Both shall be recognized leaders in the Church of God, Anderson, IN.

Section 2.2 QUALIFICATIONS Governing Board members shall be confessing Christians and live lives that reflect holiness and manifest the fruits of the spirit. They shall be well respected within their own family, their church, their profession and their community. They shall have a warm welcoming spirit, a positive attitude and be able to see the good both in people and in situations. They shall be people who possess strong visionary faith and wisdom. With the exception of the two Governing Board members who are chosen from outside of the Corporation, they shall tithe to and be regular attendees in worship at ANY Church of God, CITY, STATE. The two members chosen from outside of the Corporation shall be similarly responsible to their home church.

Section 2.3 LENGTH OF TERM Governing Board members shall be approved for a term of three years. A member who has served two consecutive full three-year terms shall not be eligible for nomination until at least one year has elapsed. Governing Board terms shall be staggered so that no more than three members have terms that end in the same year. Terms of all newly approved Governing Board members shall begin February 1.

Section 2.4 OFFICERS OF THE GOVERNING BOARD

A. Chairperson: The Chairperson shall preside at all meetings of the Governing Board. During times of transition in the Senior Pastoral leadership, the Chairperson may also call Special Business Meetings of the Corporation. The Chairperson of the Governing Board will, by virtue of his or her office, also serve as an officer of the Corporation. The Chairperson shall be a member of __________ Church of God, CITY, STATE.

B. Vice Chairperson: The Vice-Chairperson shall preside at meetings of the Governing Board in the absence of the Chairperson or if disciplinary action of the Chairperson is required. All members of the Governing Board including those members from outside the Corporation shall be eligible to serve as Vice-Chair.

C. Financial Operations Officer: The Financial Operations Officer shall be responsible for directing the dissemination of regular financial reports to the Governing Board. The Financial Operations Officer of the Governing Board shall, by the virtue of his or her office, also be the Treasurer of the Corporation. This position shall be held by a member of _____________ Church of God, CITY, STATE.

D. Secretary: The Secretary shall ensure that all minutes of the Governing Board are properly recorded and made available for future reference. The Secretary of the Governing Board shall, by virtue of his or her office, also be the Secretary of the Corporation. The Secretary shall be a member of ____ Church of God, CITY, STATE.

Section 2.5 DUTIES OF THE GOVERNING BOARD

A. To give oversight and counsel to the Senior Pastor to ensure that the Corporation is effectively accomplishing its stated purpose.

B. To hold in trust all the property of the Corporation in accordance with the laws of the State of ________.

C. To ratify the actions of the Senior Pastor, staff, lay ministry leaders and volunteers in the performance of their duties on behalf of the Corporation.

D. To approve compensation packages and leave policy for the Senior Pastor and pastoral staff.

E. To approve the hiring and dismissal of the pastoral staff. Approval shall require a three-fourths (75%) majority vote of the Governing Board.

F. To approve the proposed Annual General Operating Budget that will be presented to the Corporation for approval at the Annual Business Meeting.

G. To approve all long term debt. Long term debt in excess of three years and/or a per year amount in excess of 5% of the Annual General Operating Budget must also be approved by the Corporation.

H. To ensure that an examination of the Corporation's financial records are reviewed annually and to ensure that an audit of the records and financial procedures are completed by an independent accounting firm every four (4) years.

I. To fill any vacancies on the Leadership Selection Committee until such vacancies shall be filled by members individually ratified by the Corporation.

J. To appoint a Bylaws Committee as needed.

K. To appoint a Pulpit Committee during times of transition in the senior pastorate.

L. To oversee the processes for reconciliation, restoration and, if needed, discipline in the event that the Senior Pastor, pastoral staff, support staff, ministry leaders or any member of the Corporation is unfaithful to the trust they have been given. All action on the part of the Governing Board should be done in accordance with Biblical principles and under the guidance of the Holy Spirit. Special care should be taken to deal with the offending party in Christian love while at the same time protecting the Corporation from behavior that is or may become harmful to the Body of Christ.

M. In the event that any officer of the Corporation is unable to fulfill a portion or all of his or her stated responsibilities, the Governing Board may temporarily assign his or her duties to another officer or assume the responsibilities themselves.

Section 2.6 MEETINGS The Governing Board shall meet at least quarterly. Meetings may be in person, by phone conference or by video conference. It may establish regular meetings or schedule special meetings, as needed, to accomplish its duties. The Senior Pastor or any member of the Governing Board may call a meeting at any time, under the condition that a majority of the Governing Board' members can be present at the meeting.

Section 2.7 QUORUM A quorum shall consist of a simple majority of the Governing Board members.

Section 2.8 VOTING All votes shall be decided by a simple majority vote of Governing Board members present unless otherwise stated within the Bylaws.

Section 2.9 RESIGNATION OR DISMISSAL OF A GOVERNING BOARD MEMBER

A. Should a member of the Governing Board need to resign his or her position for any reason, he or she should submit his or her resignation in writing to the Governing Board. The resigning member should endeavor to provide a minimum of thirty days before vacating the position. In such case, the Leadership Selection Committee may appoint a successor for the position to serve until the next Annual Business Meeting of the Corporation. In no case shall the appointed member assume the role of an officer until he or she has been approved by the Corporation.

B. Should a member of the Governing Board be found to be unfaithful to his or her trust to the Corporation, the Governing Board may require his or her removal from the Governing Board. Such action shall require a three-fourths (75%) majority vote of the voting members of the Governing Board.

C. Should the Governing Board determine that the removal of a Governing Board member, for any reason, would be beneficial to the Corporation in the accomplishment of its stated purpose, it may do so by a three-fourths (75%) majority vote of the voting members of the Governing Board.

ARTICLE III. LEADERSHIP SELECTION COMMITTEE

Section 3.1 MEMBERSHIP The Leadership Selection Committee shall consist of four members recommended by the Governing Board and individually ratified by the **Corporation** plus the Senior Pastor as an ex-officio voting member. No ratified member of the Leadership Selection Committee shall serve concurrently as a member of the Governing Board. The Governing Board shall appoint the Chairperson.

Section 3.2 QUALIFICATIONS Members of the Leadership Selection Committee shall be confessing Christians and live lives that reflect holiness and manifest the fruits of the Spirit. They shall be well respected within their own family, their church, their profession and their community. They shall be people that possess wisdom and discernment.

Section 3.3 LENGTH OF TERM Members of the Leadership Selection Committee shall be appointed for a term of three years. A member who has served two consecutive terms shall not be eligible for appointment until at least one year has elapsed. If more than two Leadership Selection Committee members are being appointed in any one year, the length of terms shall be staggered so that no more than two members have terms that end in the same year.

Section 3.4 MEETINGS Meetings shall be held as needed and shall be called by the Chairperson. At least four of the five members must be present to conduct a meeting.

Section 3.5 DUTIES The duties of the Committee shall be:

A. To nominate Governing Board members chosen from within the lay membership of the Corporation.

B. To approve the nominees presented to the Leadership Selection Committee by the Senior Pastor for Governing Board members chosen from outside of the Corporation.

C. To present the names of the nominees for the Governing Board to the Corporation for approval at the Annual Business Meeting. Approval requires a three-fourths (75%) majority vote of Voting Members of the Corporation present and voting, including approved absentee ballots.

D. To ensure that a sample ballot shall be made available to the Corporation at least two weeks prior to the Annual Business Meeting.

E. All nominations, ratifications and appointments made by the Leadership Selection Committee must be unanimous decisions of the Committee members present.

ARTICLE IV. BYLAWS COMMITTEE

Section 4.1 MEMBERSHIP The Bylaws Committee shall consist of four members from within the Corporation appointed by the Governing Board, plus the Senior Pastor as ex-officio member. The Governing Board shall appoint a chairperson.

Section 4.2 QUALIFICATIONS Members of the Bylaws Committee shall be confessing Christians and live lives that reflect holiness and manifest the fruits of the Spirit. They shall be well respected within their own family, their church, their profession and their community. They shall be people that possess wisdom and discernment.

Section 4.3 MEETINGS Meetings shall be held as needed and shall be called by the Chairperson. A majority of members must be present to conduct a meeting.

Section 4.4 DUTIES The duties of the Committee shall be:

A. To review the present Constitution and Bylaws and identify issues to be addressed.

B. To propose to the Corporation any changes that the Committee determines are needed. These proposed changes may alter, amend, replace or repeal the present Constitution and/or Bylaws.

C. Copies of the proposed amendments shall be made available at least two weeks prior to the informational meeting(s) along with the Article(s) and Section(s) to be altered, amended, replaced or repealed.

Section 4.5 TERM The Bylaws Committee shall be dissolved after the approval of the proposed Constitution and/or Bylaws by the Corporation. Should the proposed Constitution and/or Bylaws fail to receive the approval of the Corporation, the Governing Board shall determine the status of the Bylaws Committee.

ARTICLE V. PULPIT COMMITTEE

Section 5.1 OCCASION AND MEMBERSHIP In the event the Corporation is without the services of a Senior Pastor, a Pulpit Committee, consisting of five to seven members from within the Corporation, shall be appointed by the Governing Board, of which three or more members of the Pulpit Committee shall be selected from the Governing Board. The Governing Board shall designate the Chairperson of the Committee. The Chairperson of the Pulpit Committee shall meet regularly with the Governing Board during the interim period. The Governing Board shall also choose a pastor who is a recognized leader within the Church of God, Anderson, IN to serve as Counseling Pastor to the Committee. The Counseling Pastor may come from the membership of the Governing Board.

Section 5.2 QUALIFICATIONS Members of the Pulpit Committee shall be confessing Christians and live lives that reflect holiness and manifest the fruits of the Spirit. They shall be well respected within their own family, their church, their profession and their community. They shall be people that possess strong visionary faith, wisdom and discernment.

Section 5.3 DUTIES

A. The Pulpit Committee shall be responsible for the regular services during the period when the Corporation is without senior pastoral leadership. They shall communicate and work with staff in carrying out this responsibility.

B. The Pulpit Committee shall investigate the availability of prospective pastors who are ordained by the Church of God, Anderson IN. The Committee shall study their qualifications as to character, leadership abilities, experience, ministerial recognition and status.

C. The Pulpit Committee shall submit the name of only one prospective Senior Pastor at a time to the Corporation for consideration and possible call. Approval by the Corporation requires a three-fourths (75%) majority vote of Voting Members present and voting at a Business Meeting, including approved absentee ballots.

D. The Pulpit Committee shall arrange with the ratified Senior Pastor and ministers of the area for a Service of Installation that will add dignity to the call and express the Corporation's recognition of his or her leadership.

Section 5.4 TERM The Pulpit Committee shall be dissolved upon completion of the Installation Service.

ARTICLE VI. RESIGNATION OR DISMISSAL OF A SENIOR PASTOR

Section 6.1 RESIGNATION

A. Should the Senior Pastor feel led by the Holy Spirit to terminate his or her pastoral leadership role in the Corporation, he or she shall present a written resignation to the Governing Board. The Senior Pastor should endeavor to provide a minimum of sixty days before vacating the pastorate, unless other arrangements are made to the satisfaction of both the Governing Board and the Senior Pastor.

B. Should the Governing Board feel led by the Holy Spirit that a change of Senior Pastoral leadership is needed in order for the Corporation to accomplish its stated purpose, they may ask for the resignation of the Senior Pastor. Such action would require a two-thirds vote of the voting members of the Governing Board. The Senior Pastor should be provided a minimum of sixty days before vacating the pastorate, unless other arrangements are made to the satisfaction of both the Governing Board and the Senior Pastor.

Section 6.2 DISMISSAL

A. If the Senior Pastor were considered to be unfaithful to his or her trust to the Corporation or refused a request for resignation made by the Governing Board, the Governing Board may require his or her dismissal. Such action would require a two-thirds vote of the voting members of the Governing Board and should be done in an attitude of Christian love and under the guidance of the Holy Spirit.

B. If a member of the Corporation believes that the Senior Pastor has been unfaithful to his or her trust to the Corporation, he or she may take the matter to any member of the Governing Board. If the claim has merit, the Governing Board shall respond accordingly. Other issues or concerns, not involving a breech of trust, should first be taken directly to the Senior Pastor in keeping with Matthew 18:15.

Section 6.3 APPEAL PROCESS If the Senior Pastor wishes to appeal a decision for dismissal made by the Governing Board, the matter can be taken to the Credentials Committee of the STATE Ministries of the Church of God, Anderson, IN for assistance and possible reconciliation.

ARTICLE VII. BUSINESS MEETINGS

Section 7.1 PROCESS All Business Meetings of the Corporation shall be preceded by an informational meeting(s), in which all items to be voted on will be presented and an opportunity provided for questions and open discussion. No votes shall take place at the informational meeting and no Quorum will be required. The Business Meeting shall take place at least one week after the informational meeting(s) and shall consist of a congregational vote, with limited discussion from the floor, on each item being presented for consideration. Discussion shall be limited to questions for clarification on the matters subject to a vote. A quorum shall be required for the Business Meeting. Minutes of the Business Meeting shall be reviewed by the officers of the Corporation and approved at the next Business Meeting.

Section 7.2 TIME OF BUSINESS MEETINGS In order to secure the broadest possible participation in the Business Meetings, all Business Meetings shall be held in conjunction with the weekend worship services of the Corporation. In the event of multiple weekend worship services, different sessions of the same Business Meeting may be held in order to provide more than one opportunity for Corporation members to cast their ballots.

Section 7.3 VOTING Each voting member of the Corporation shall be entitled to one vote on each question at any Business Meeting of the Corporation. Unless otherwise required in these Bylaws or the Constitution of the Corporation, all questions at any meeting having a Quorum shall be decided by a three-fourths (75%) vote. All voting members of the Corporation participating in any Business Meeting of the Corporation shall be required to register at the meeting in which they are voting. The names of those registered voters shall become a part of the minutes of the meeting. The Chairperson of the Business Meeting shall appoint tellers to count the votes. The results of the vote shall become a part of the minutes of the meeting.

Section 7.4 ABSENTEE BALLOT In the event a voting member of the Corporation will not be present for a Business Meeting, he or she may cast an absentee ballot, provided it has been requested prior to the meeting. Each marked ballot must be sealed in an envelope bearing the voter's name and returned to an officer of the Corporation, or an official designee, before the meeting. The list of absentee voters shall be approved by the Officers of the Corporation. The list of absentee voters shall be recorded in the minutes of the Business Meeting at which their votes are cast.

Section 7.5 QUORUM All Business Meetings shall require a quorum of Corporation members participating in the vote in order for the vote to be official. A quorum for any Business Meeting shall consist of sixty (60) percent of the active registered voters. Members who have voted within the last two years are considered active unless otherwise disqualified. Absentee ballots and ballots cast by present voting members shall be used in determining a quorum. A quorum shall be determined only after all ballots have been tallied. In the event that a quorum is not achieved, the results shall remain secret and the Business Meeting shall be reconvened within thirty days. If after thirty days a quorum is still not achieved, the vote shall be void and the matter returned to the Governing Board for consideration.

Section 7.6 FISCAL YEAR The fiscal year for financial records shall be the calendar year.

Section 7.7 ANNUAL BUSINESS MEETING The Annual Business Meeting of the Corporation shall be held each year during the month of January.

Section 7.8 SPECIAL BUSINESS MEETINGS Special Business Meetings of the Corporation may be called for one or more stated purposes by the Senior Pastor. During the interim period between Senior Pastorates, Special Business Meetings may be called by the Chairperson of the Governing Board.

Section 7.9 NOTICE OF MEETINGS Notice of all Business Meetings of the Corporation shall be given at least two weeks in advance of the informational meeting(s). The purpose, date, time and place of both the informational meeting(s) and the Business Meeting shall be given in the notice.

ARTICLE VIII. FINANCIAL GUIDELINES

Section 8.1 BASIS FOR ANNUAL GENERAL OPERATING BUDGET The Annual General Operating Budget of the Corporation shall be presented by the Senior Pastor to the Governing Board for approval and then to the entire Corporation for approval at its Annual Business Meeting. Any additional annual budgets established for particular ministries of the Corporation or for specific designated causes shall be dealt with separately and shall require only the approval of the Governing Board.

Section 8.2 EXPENDITURES

A. Budgeted amounts are not to be considered actual monies available. All expenditures of budgeted monies must be approved by the Senior Pastor. He or she may at any time delegate all or part of the approval process to appropriate staff and/or ministry leaders.

B. Any undesignated income received over and above the General Operating Budget within the current fiscal year may be utilized to enable the Corporation to accomplish its stated purpose. These expenditures shall be approved by the Senior Pastor. The total of all expenditures of undesignated income in excess of three (3) percent over the General Operating Budget for the current fiscal year shall require the approval of the Governing Board. The total of all expenditures of undesignated income in excess of fifteen (15) percent over the General Operating Budget for the current fiscal year shall require the approval of the Corporation.

C. Any undesignated funds accumulated from previous fiscal years may be used to enable the Corporation to accomplish its stated purpose. These expenditures shall be approved by the Governing Board.

ARTICLE IX. ENABLING CLAUSE

These revised Constitution and Bylaws shall become effective following their adoption by the Corporation and shall supersede any and all other Bylaws and Agreements. The date of adoption shall be recorded below and certified by the Secretary of the Corporation.

BIBLIOGRAPHY

Byrum, Russell R. *Problems of the Local Church: A Manual of the Principles and Practice of Local Churches.* Anderson, IN: Gospel Trumpet Company, 1927.

Chait, Richard, William Ryan, and Barbara Taylor. *Governance as Leadership: Reframing the Work of Nonprofit Boards*. Hoboken, NJ: John Wiley & Sons, 2005.

Hammar, Richard. "What Are Church Bylaws?" Adapted from "Governing Well" (2009) in *Church Law & Tax Report* (June 2015). https://www.churchlawandtax.com/blog/2015/june/what-are-church-bylaws.html

"How the D-Day Invasion Was Planned." *Popular Mechanics*, August 1944.

Kaiser, Dr. John, Thomas G. Bandy, and Bill Easum. *Winning on Purpose: How to Organize Congregations to Succeed in Their Mission.* Nashville: Abingdon Press, 2006. Kindle edition.

Olsen, Charles M. "A Kinder, Gentler Board Meeting." In *Growing Your Church through Training and Motivation: 30 Strategies to Transform Your Ministry*, 167–68. Edited by Marshall Shelley. Minneapolis: Bethany House, 1997.

Olsen, Charles M. *Transforming Church Boards into Communities of Spiritual Leaders.* Herndon, VA: The Alban Institute, 1995. Kindle edition.

Osborne, Larry W. *The Unity Factor: Getting Your Church Leaders Working Together.* Carol Stream, IL: Christianity Today, 1989.

Stafford, Rod. Free to Lead: *The Decision-making Ethos of Healthy Growing Churches*. Fairfax, VA: Self-Published, 2011.

Sterner, R. Eugene. *You Have a Ministry.* Anderson, IN: Warner Press, 1963.

Robert L. Moss is senior pastor of Hope Community Church in Niles, Michigan and an Executive Leader at Church of God Ministries (Anderson). He has served for more than thirty-five years in pastoral ministry, including congregations in Washington state, Wyoming, Ohio and again in Michigan. He also served as the executive state minister for more than 130 congregations in Indiana and led with distinction as a two-term chairman of the North American General Assembly of the Church of God. His ministry nationally and internationally has provided rich perspective for the creation of this book.

www.ingramcontent.com/pod-product-compliance
Lightning Source LLC
LaVergne TN
LVHW050253010825
817285LV00001B/9